FAT

Regina Hofer

graphic mundi

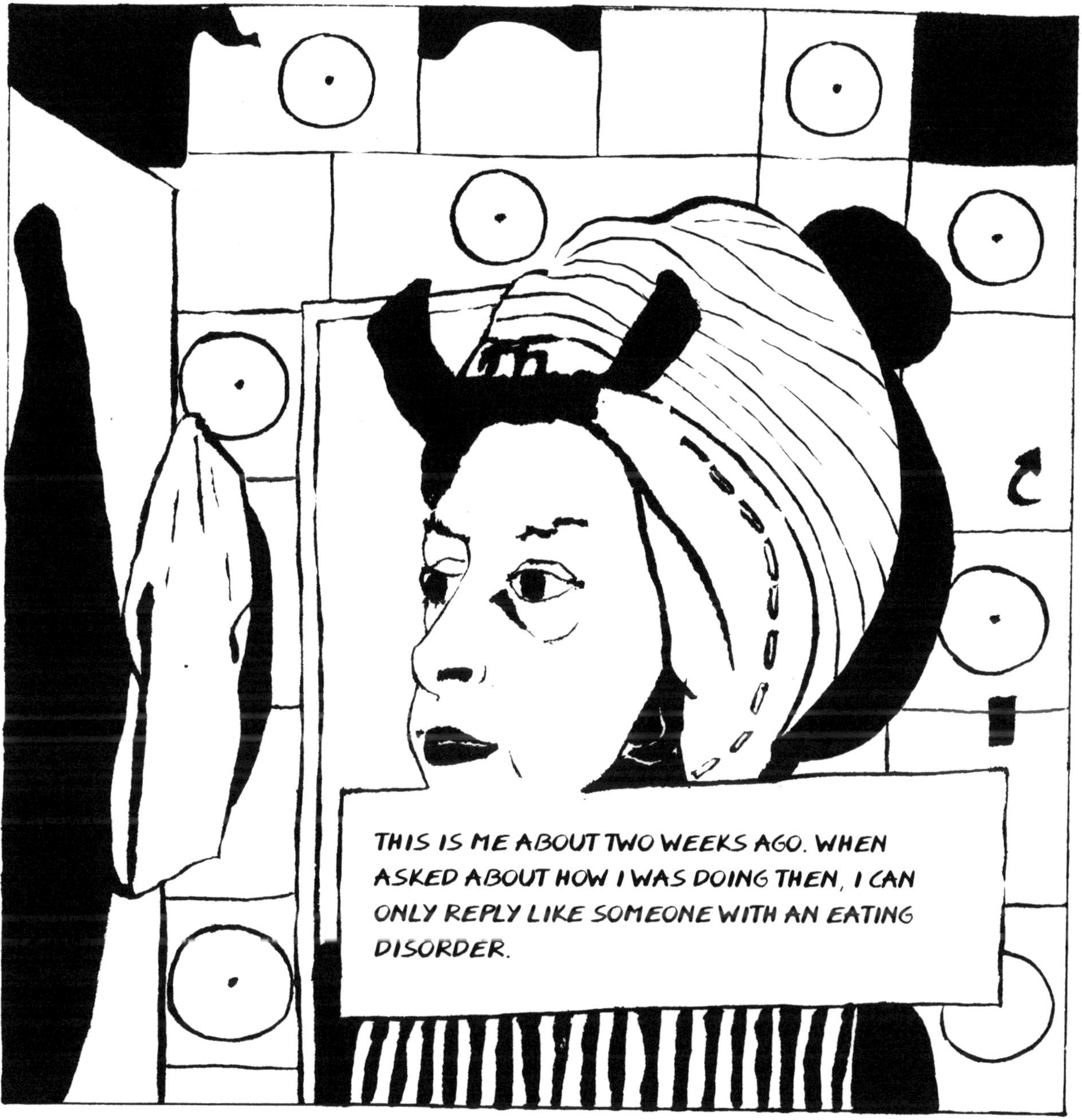
THIS IS ME ABOUT TWO WEEKS AGO. WHEN ASKED ABOUT HOW I WAS DOING THEN, I CAN ONLY REPLY LIKE SOMEONE WITH AN EATING DISORDER.

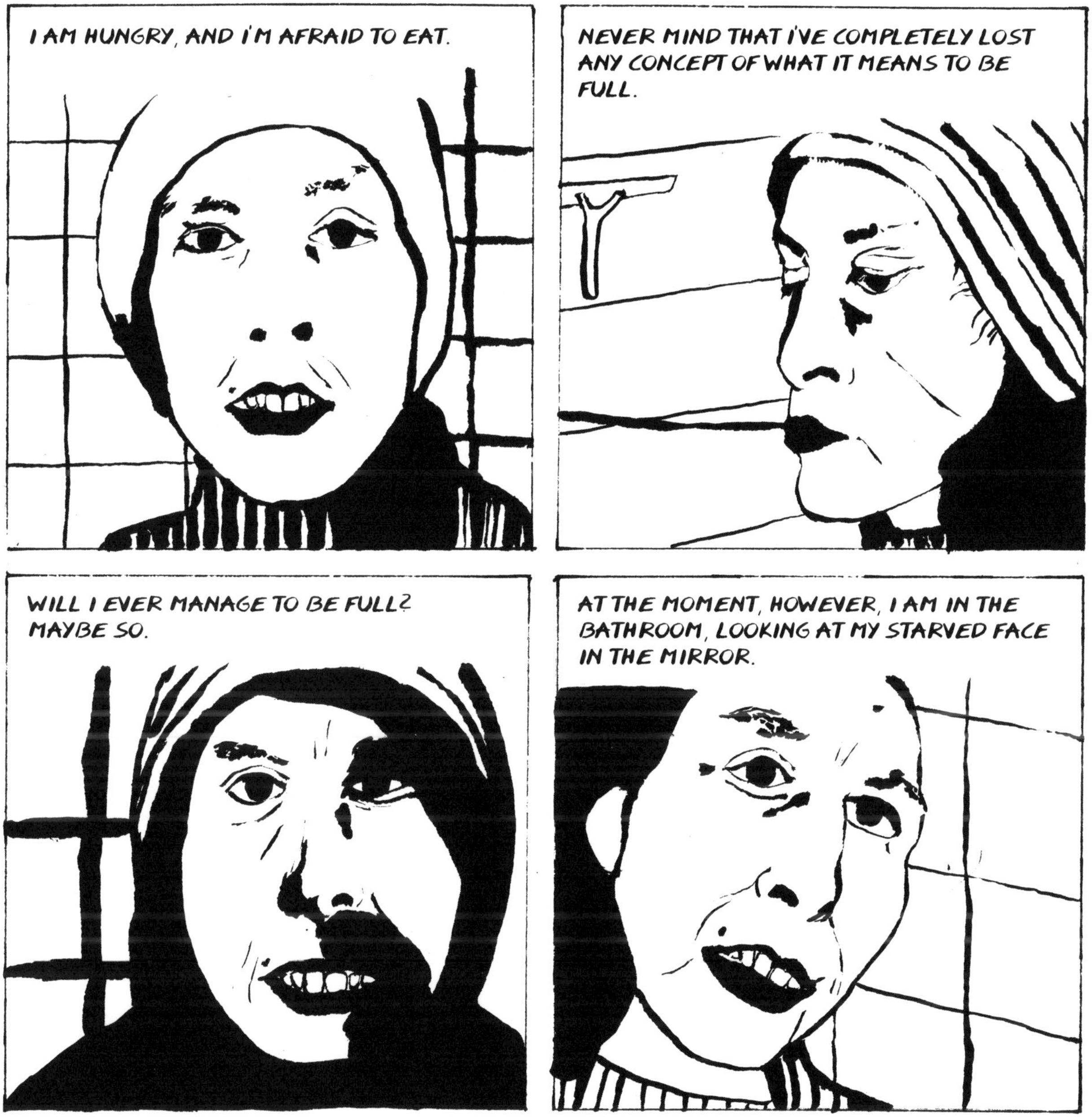
I AM HUNGRY, AND I'M AFRAID TO EAT.
NEVER MIND THAT I'VE COMPLETELY LOST ANY CONCEPT OF WHAT IT MEANS TO BE FULL.
WILL I EVER MANAGE TO BE FULL? MAYBE SO.
AT THE MOMENT, HOWEVER, I AM IN THE BATHROOM, LOOKING AT MY STARVED FACE IN THE MIRROR.

WHAT ALL ANOREXICS HAVE IN COMMON ARE THE BIG, RESTLESS EYES ...

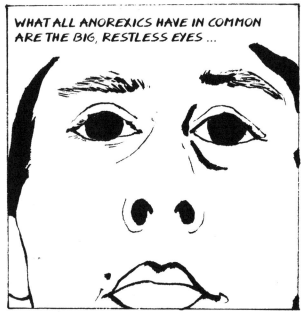

... THE FINE HAIR ON THE SKIN, WHAT'S KNOWN AS LANUGO ...

... THE UNCOORDINATED MOVEMENTS ...

... AND THE EXCESSIVE INTEREST IN OTHER PEOPLE'S SATIETY.

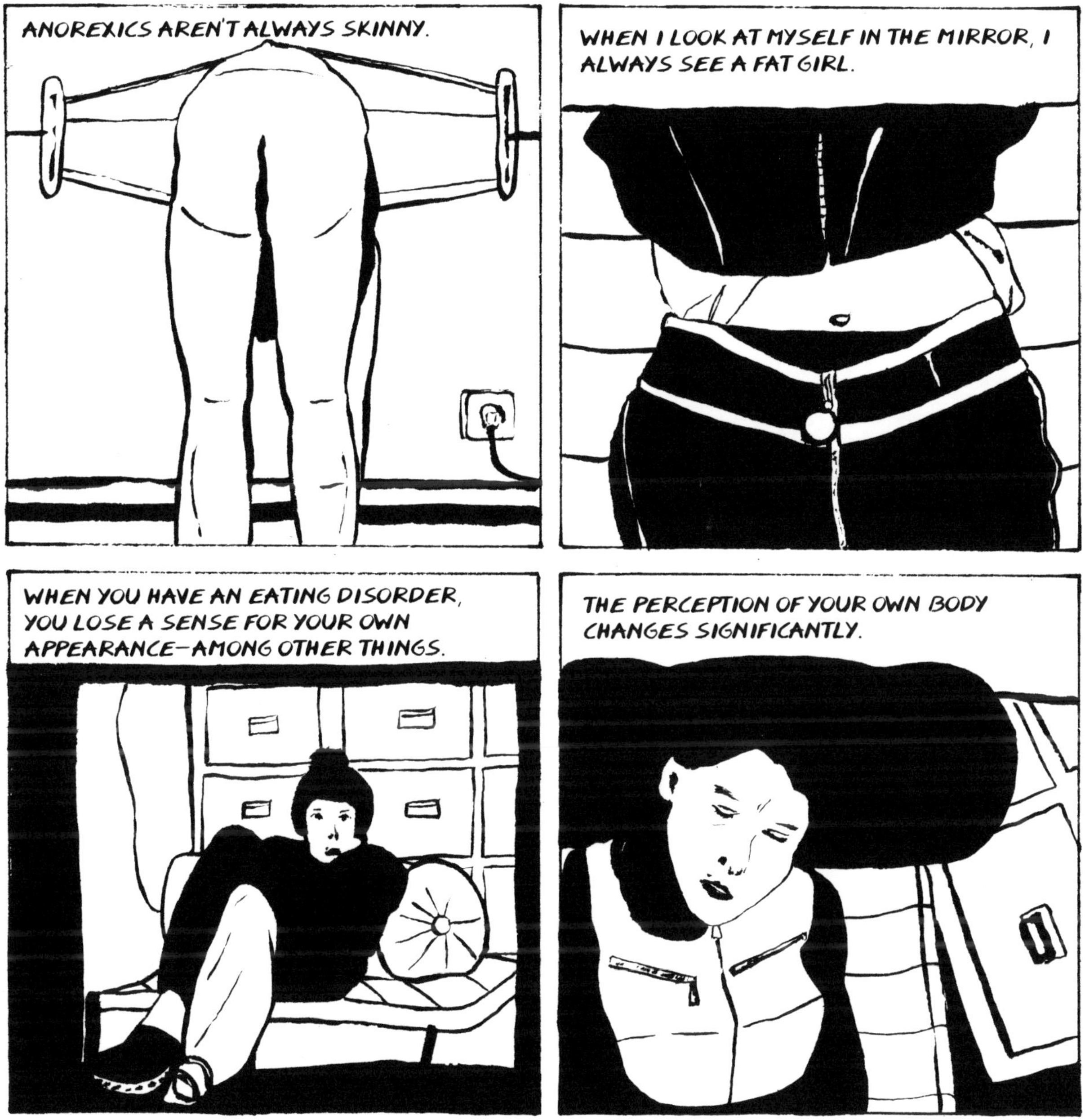
ANOREXICS AREN'T ALWAYS SKINNY.
WHEN I LOOK AT MYSELF IN THE MIRROR, I ALWAYS SEE A FAT GIRL.
WHEN YOU HAVE AN EATING DISORDER, YOU LOSE A SENSE FOR YOUR OWN APPEARANCE—AMONG OTHER THINGS.
THE PERCEPTION OF YOUR OWN BODY CHANGES SIGNIFICANTLY.

IT ALL STARTED WHEN I WAS 15 YEARS OLD.

BUT MEMORIES OF NOT FEELING COMFORTABLE IN MY OWN BODY GO BACK TO MY EARLY CHILDHOOD.

SUCH A GOOD EATER!

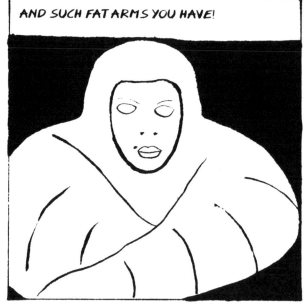

AND SUCH FAT ARMS YOU HAVE!

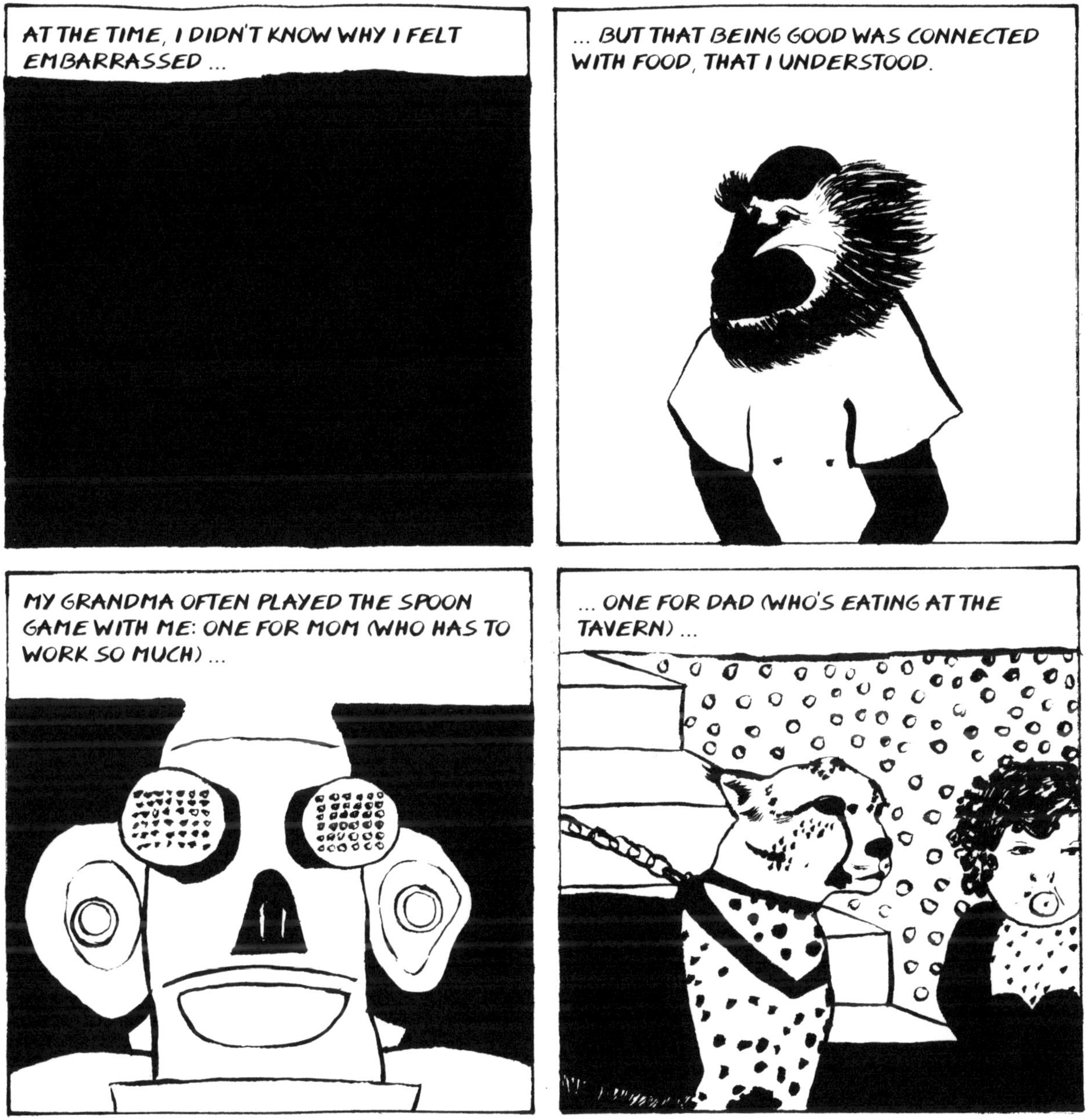
AT THE TIME, I DIDN'T KNOW WHY I FELT EMBARRASSED ...
... BUT THAT BEING GOOD WAS CONNECTED WITH FOOD, THAT I UNDERSTOOD.
MY GRANDMA OFTEN PLAYED THE SPOON GAME WITH ME: ONE FOR MOM (WHO HAS TO WORK SO MUCH) ...
... ONE FOR DAD (WHO'S EATING AT THE TAVERN) ...

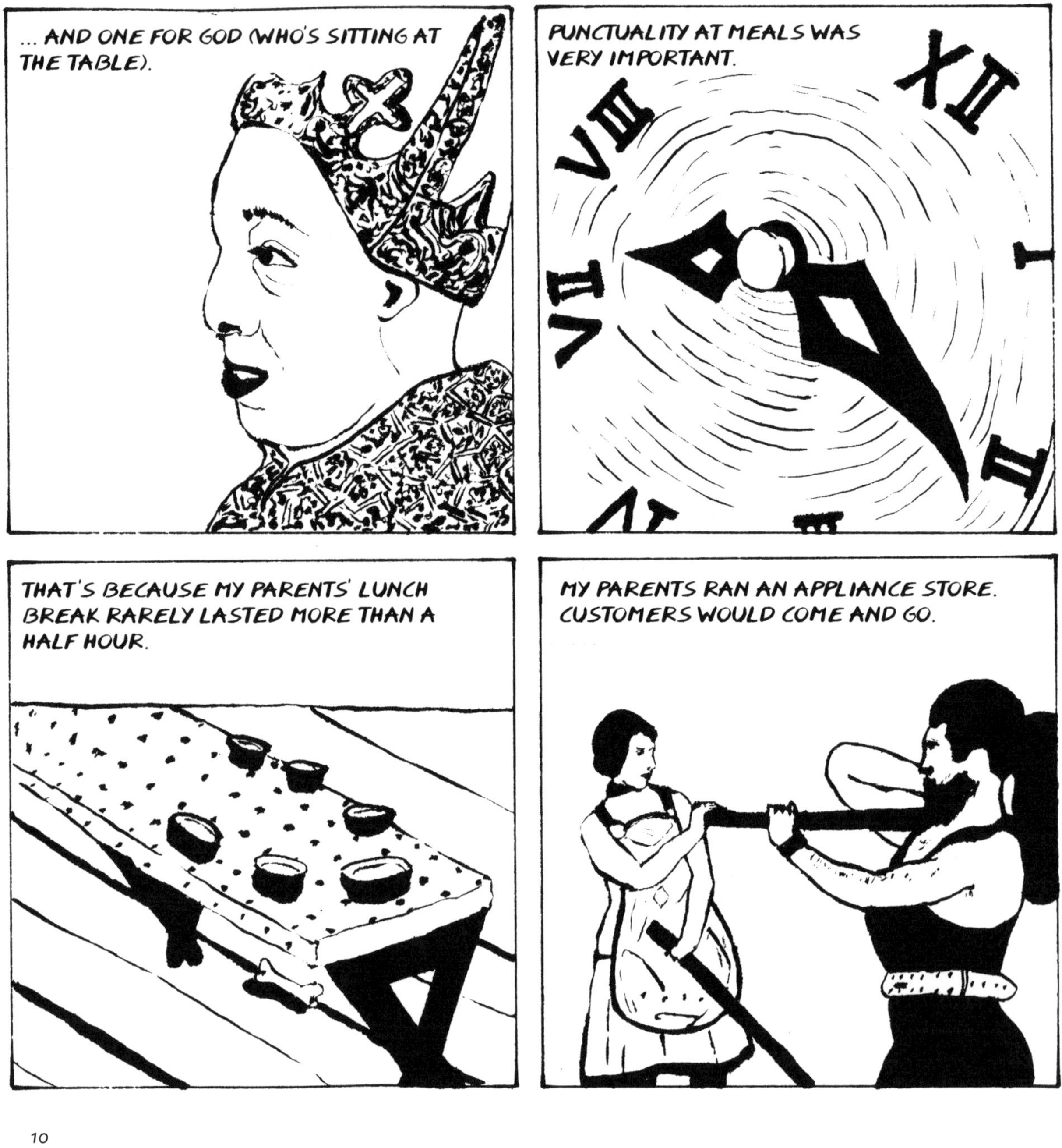
... AND ONE FOR GOD (WHO'S SITTING AT THE TABLE).
PUNCTUALITY AT MEALS WAS VERY IMPORTANT.
THAT'S BECAUSE MY PARENTS' LUNCH BREAK RARELY LASTED MORE THAN A HALF HOUR.
MY PARENTS RAN AN APPLIANCE STORE. CUSTOMERS WOULD COME AND GO.

MY MOTHER GOT PREGNANT AT EIGHTEEN.

MY FATHER WAS 28.

EVEN DURING THEIR HONEYMOON, MY DAD WOULD GO TO THE TAVERN WITHOUT MY MOTHER.

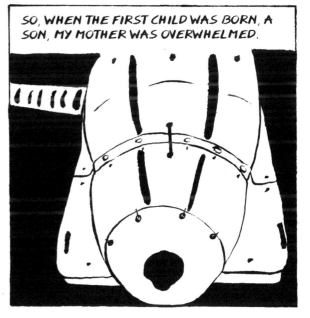

SO, WHEN THE FIRST CHILD WAS BORN, A SON, MY MOTHER WAS OVERWHELMED.

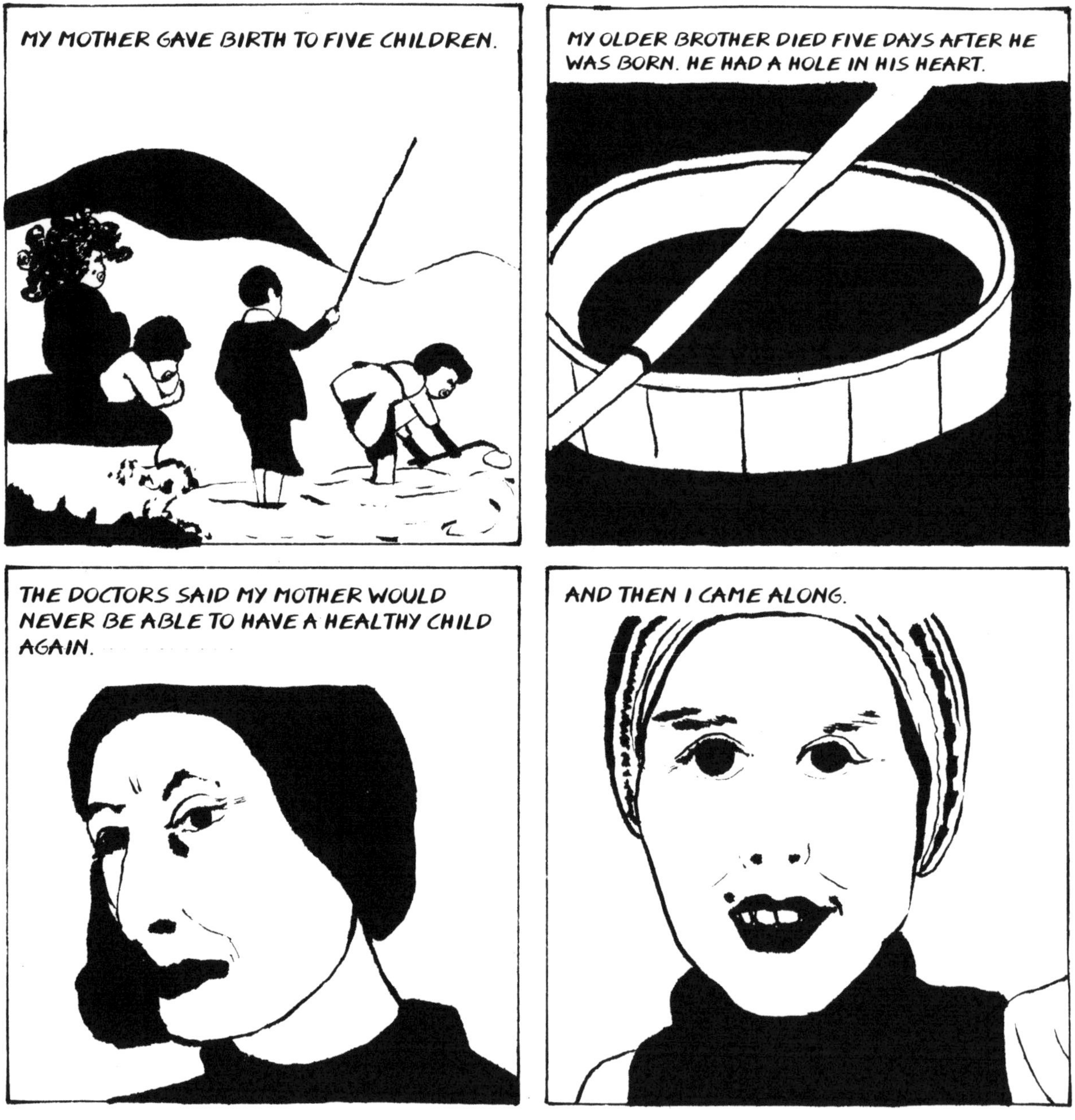
MY MOTHER GAVE BIRTH TO FIVE CHILDREN.
MY OLDER BROTHER DIED FIVE DAYS AFTER HE WAS BORN. HE HAD A HOLE IN HIS HEART.
THE DOCTORS SAID MY MOTHER WOULD NEVER BE ABLE TO HAVE A HEALTHY CHILD AGAIN.
AND THEN I CAME ALONG.

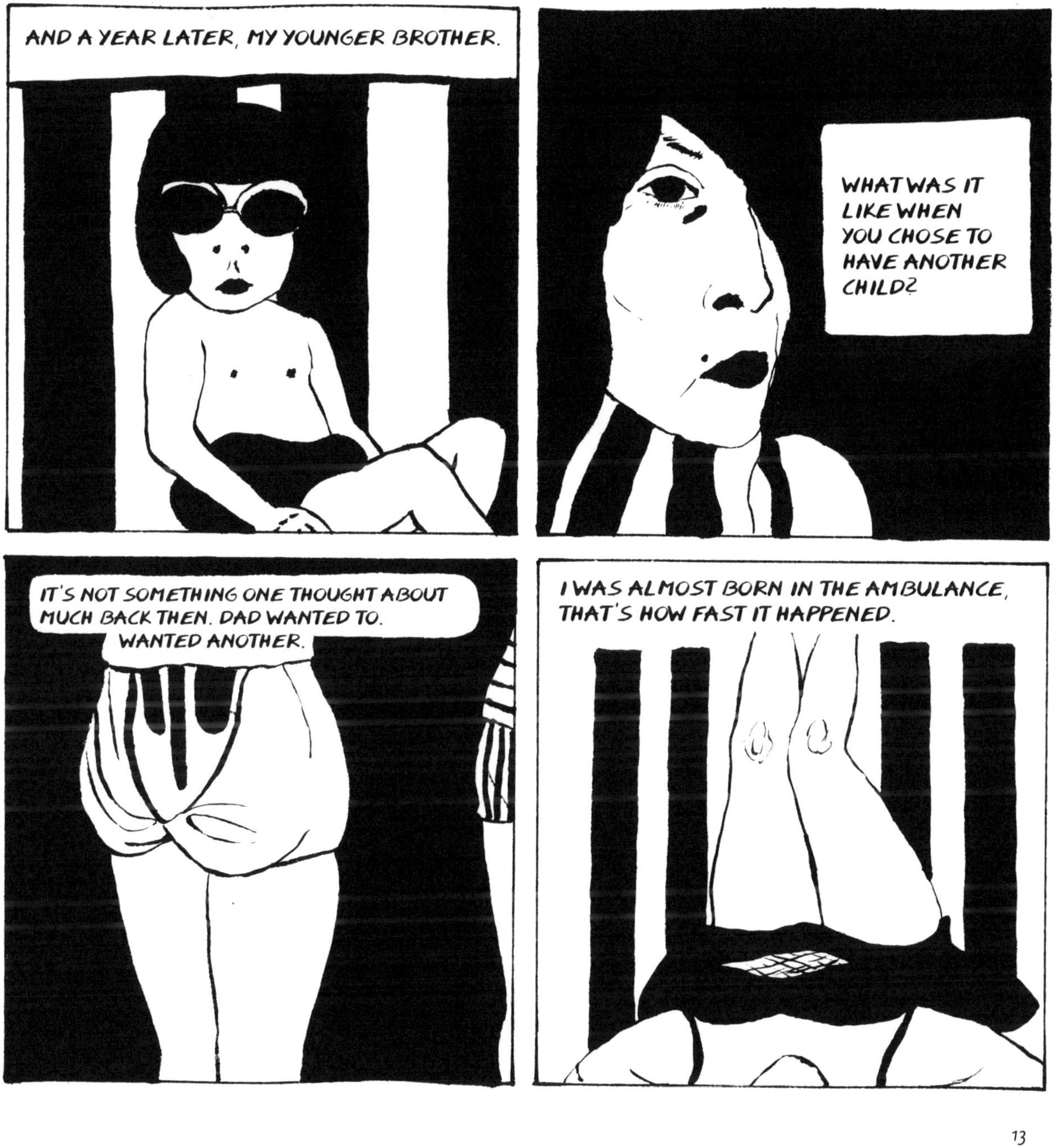
AND A YEAR LATER, MY YOUNGER BROTHER.
WHAT WAS IT LIKE WHEN YOU CHOSE TO HAVE ANOTHER CHILD?
IT'S NOT SOMETHING ONE THOUGHT ABOUT MUCH BACK THEN. DAD WANTED TO. WANTED ANOTHER.
I WAS ALMOST BORN IN THE AMBULANCE, THAT'S HOW FAST IT HAPPENED.

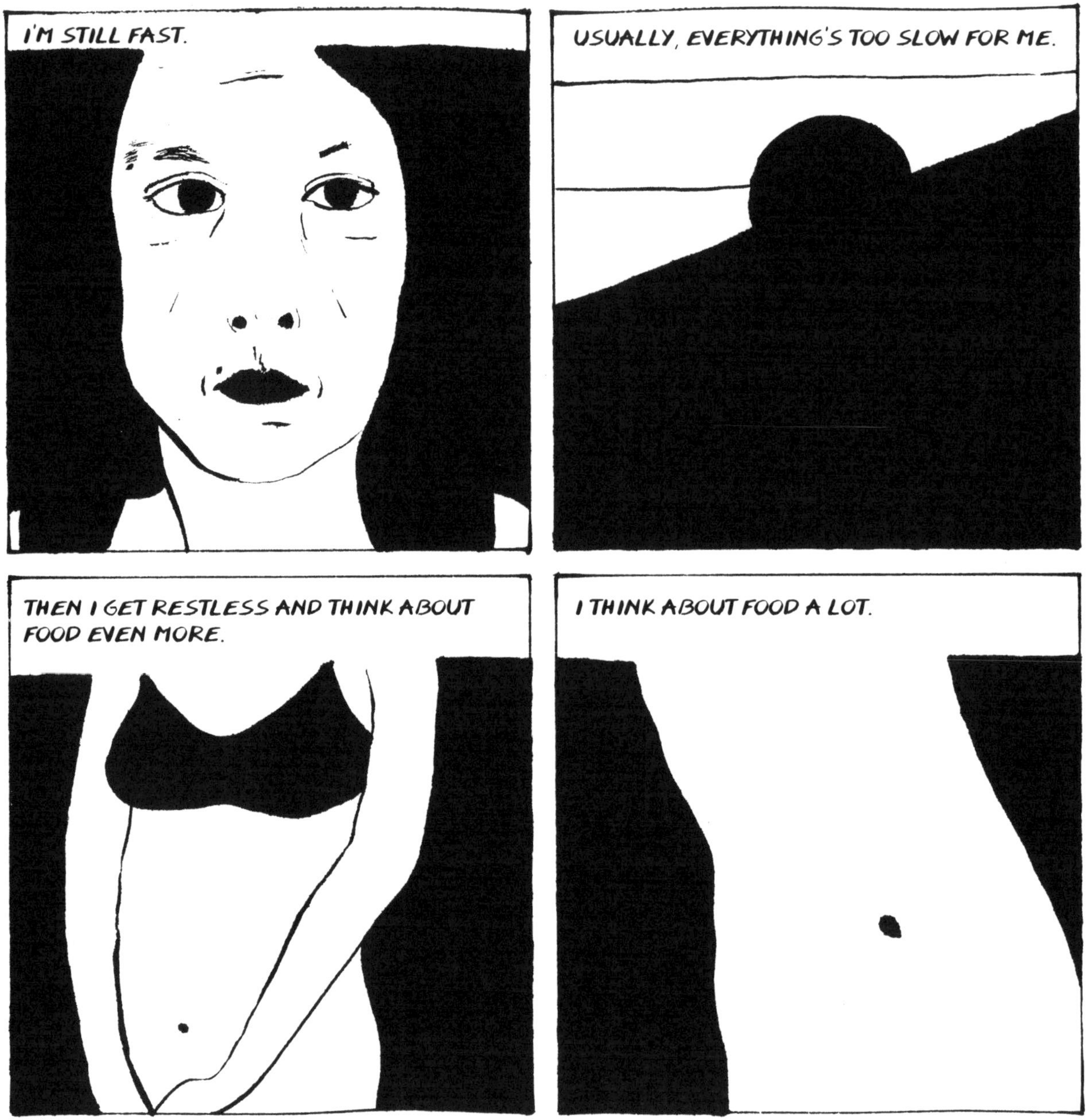
I'M STILL FAST.
USUALLY, EVERYTHING'S TOO SLOW FOR ME.
THEN I GET RESTLESS AND THINK ABOUT FOOD EVEN MORE.
I THINK ABOUT FOOD A LOT.

WHAT I AM ALLOWED TO EAT TODAY ...

... WHETHER I CAN EAT TODAY, OR HOW MUCH I CAN EAT.

I WOULD PREFER NOT TO HAVE TO EAT AT ALL.

BUT I'M USED TO THAT.

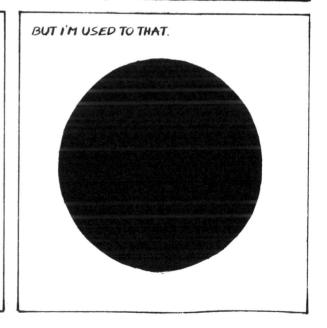

WHEN I WAS SIXTEEN, I STARTED CUTTING BACK ON MEALS, MORE AND MORE.

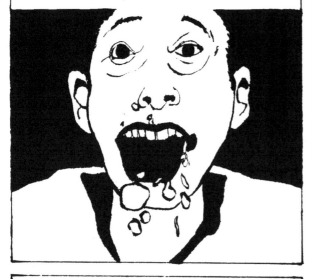

PRETTY SOON, I WAS EATING ONLY A COUPLE OF SLICES OF TOAST AND AN APPLE A DAY.

I DRANK FAR TOO LITTLE, TOO.

AND I STARTED DOING VERY POORLY AT SCHOOL.

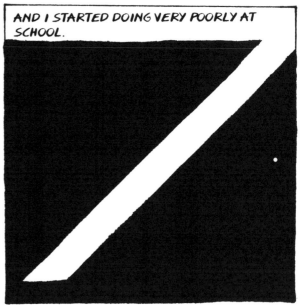

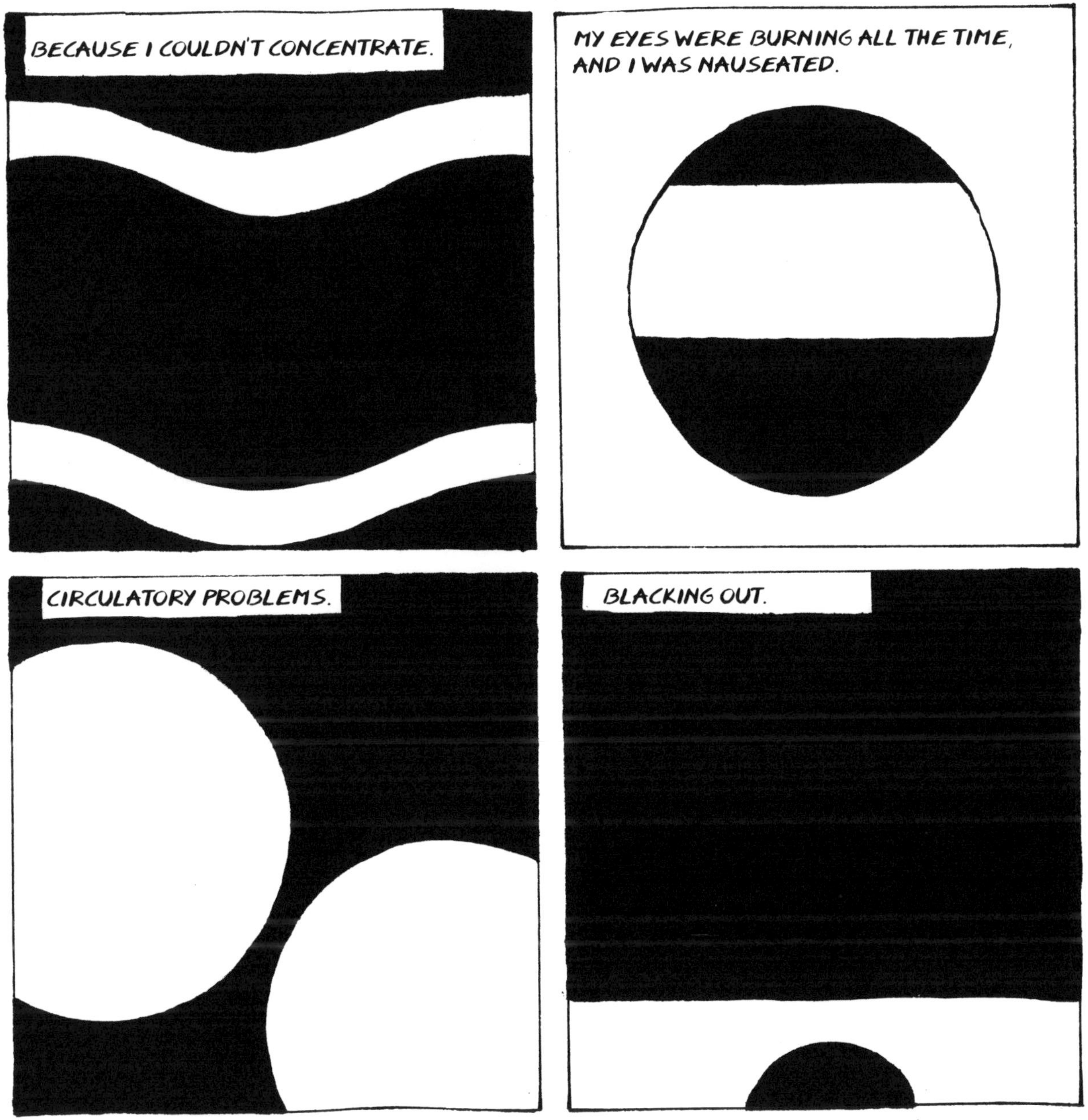
BECAUSE I COULDN'T CONCENTRATE.
MY EYES WERE BURNING ALL THE TIME, AND I WAS NAUSEATED.
CIRCULATORY PROBLEMS.
BLACKING OUT.

I WAS ABLE TO KEEP ALL OF THIS A SECRET FOR A PRETTY LONG TIME.

BUT WHEN MY HAIR STARTED FALLING OUT, THAT'S WHEN I GOT SCARED.

YOUR BREASTS ARE SHRIVELING UP!

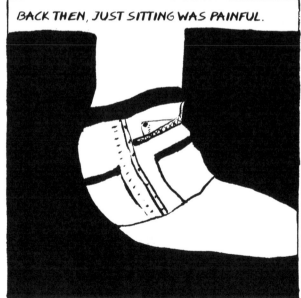

BACK THEN, JUST SITTING WAS PAINFUL.

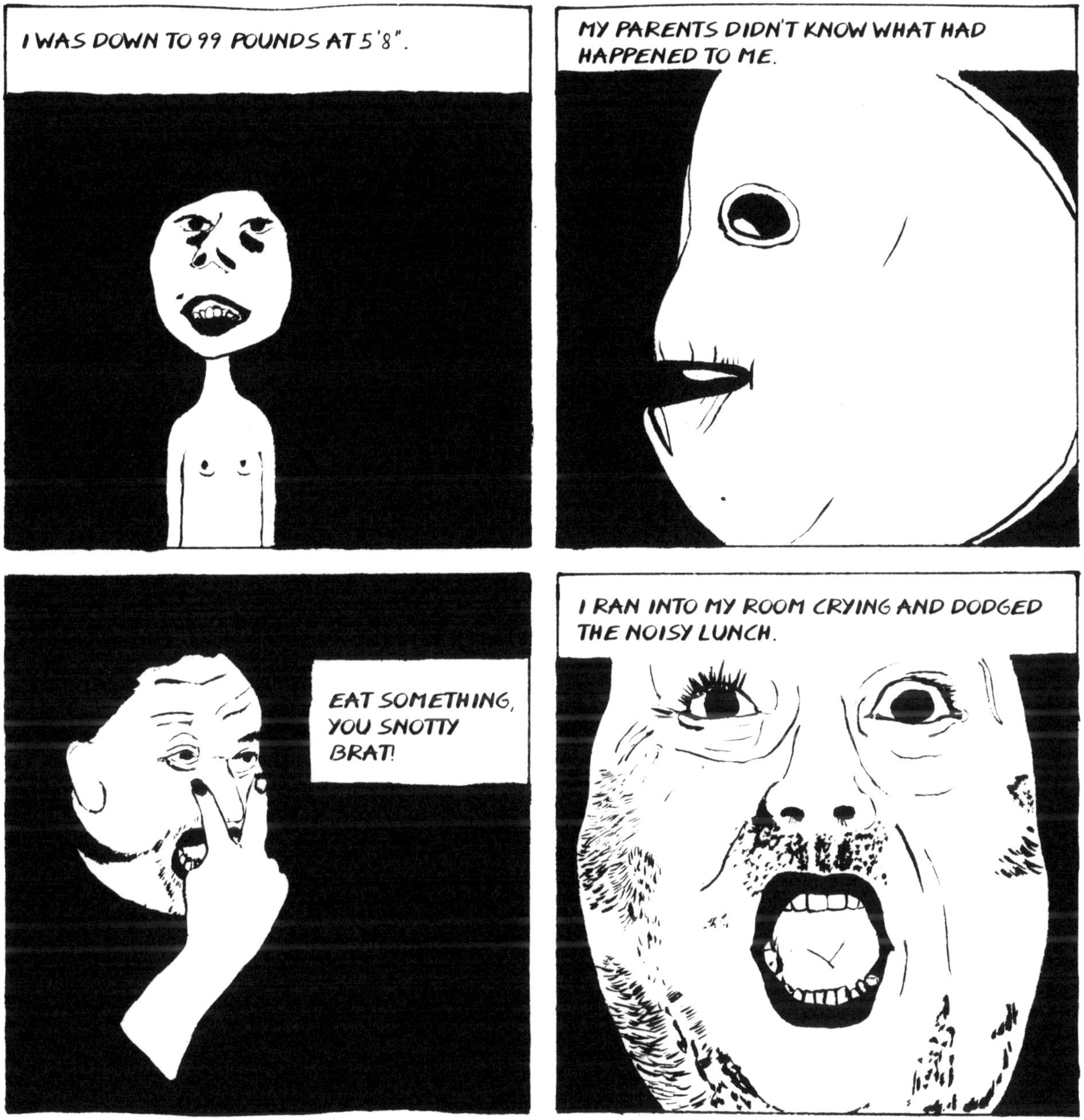
I WAS DOWN TO 99 POUNDS AT 5'8".
MY PARENTS DIDN'T KNOW WHAT HAD HAPPENED TO ME.
EAT SOMETHING, YOU SNOTTY BRAT!
I RAN INTO MY ROOM CRYING AND DODGED THE NOISY LUNCH.

AFTER THE ANOREXIA, I STARTED BINGEING.

HUNGER WON OUT, AND I STARTED TO EAT. IN SECRET.

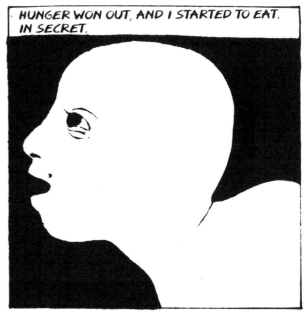

I ATE BENEATH MY BED.

AT NIGHT, WHEN EVERYONE WAS ASLEEP.

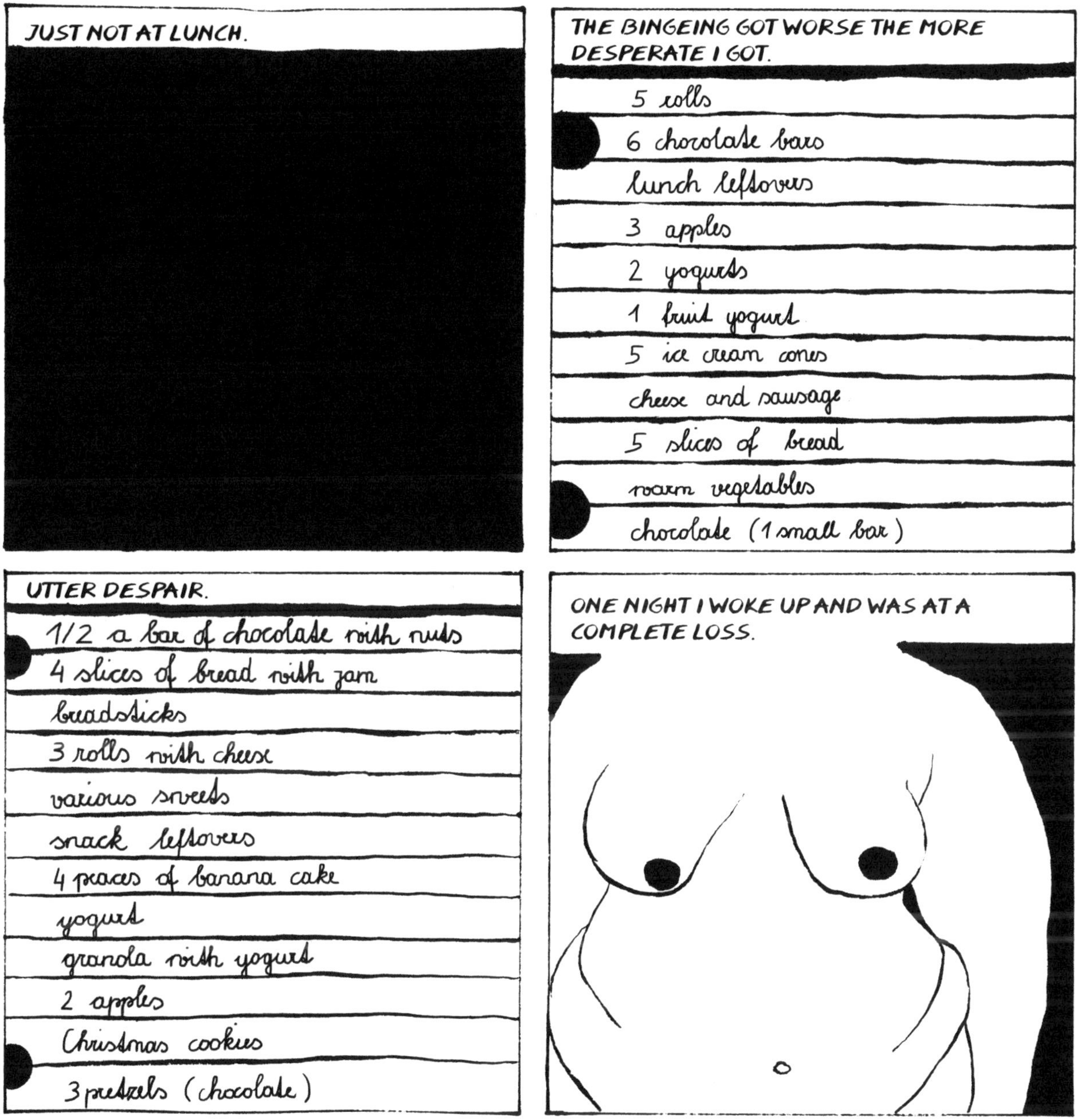
JUST NOT AT LUNCH.
THE BINGEING GOT WORSE THE MORE DESPERATE I GOT.
5 rolls
6 chocolate bars
lunch leftovers
3 apples
2 yogurts
1 fruit yogurt
5 ice cream cones
cheese and sausage
5 slices of bread
warm vegetables
chocolate (1 small bar)
UTTER DESPAIR.
1/2 a bar of chocolate with nuts
4 slices of bread with jam
breadsticks
3 rolls with cheese
various sweets
snack leftovers
4 pieces of banana cake
yogurt
granola with yogurt
2 apples
Christmas cookies
3 pretzels (chocolate)
ONE NIGHT I WOKE UP AND WAS AT A COMPLETE LOSS.

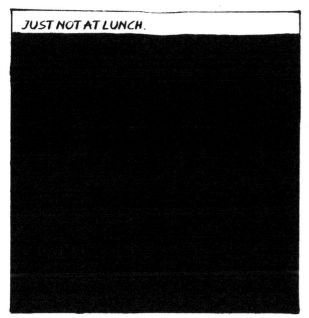

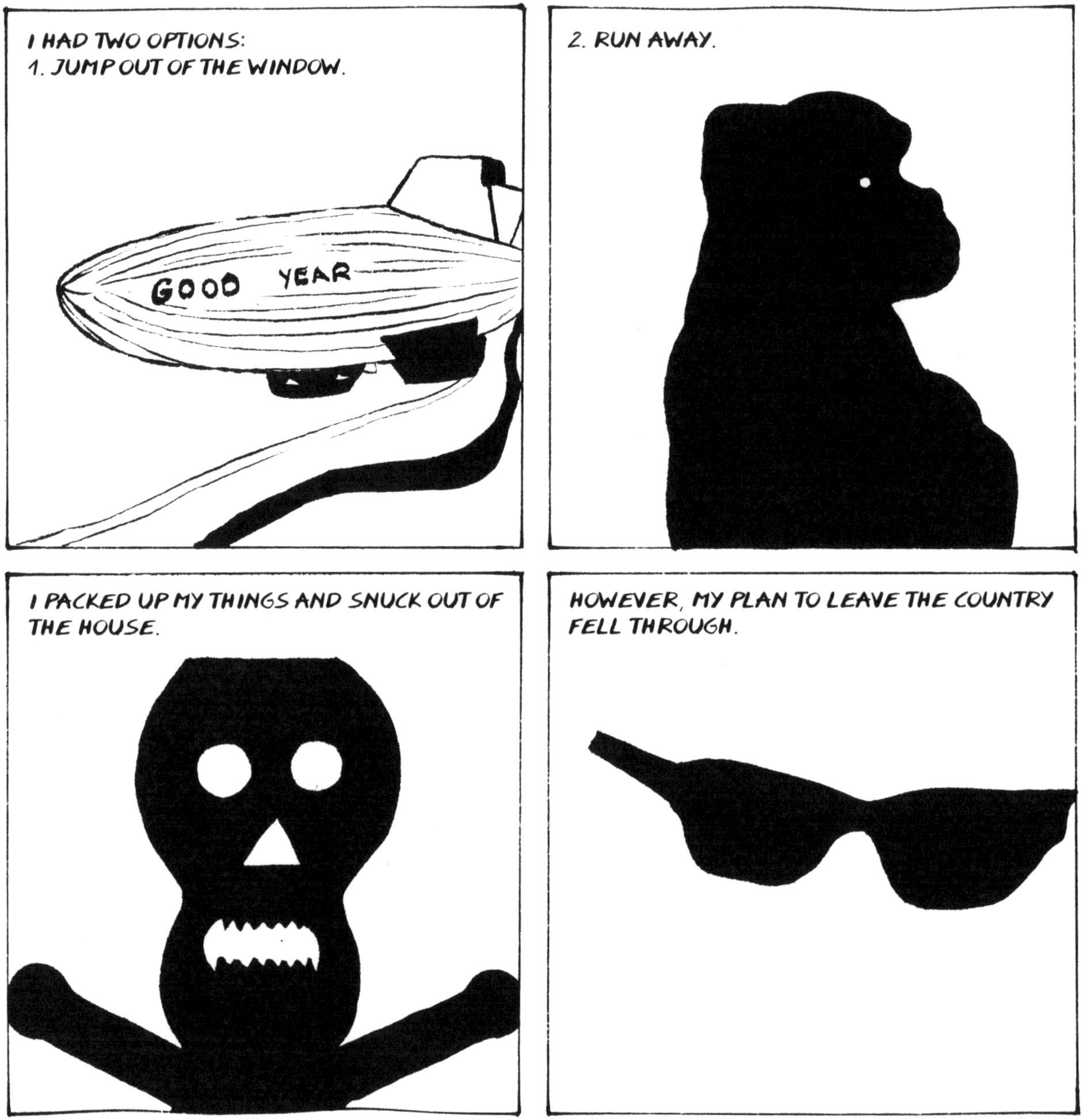
I HAD TWO OPTIONS:
1. JUMP OUT OF THE WINDOW.
GOOD YEAR
2. RUN AWAY.
I PACKED UP MY THINGS AND SNUCK OUT OF THE HOUSE.
HOWEVER, MY PLAN TO LEAVE THE COUNTRY FELL THROUGH.

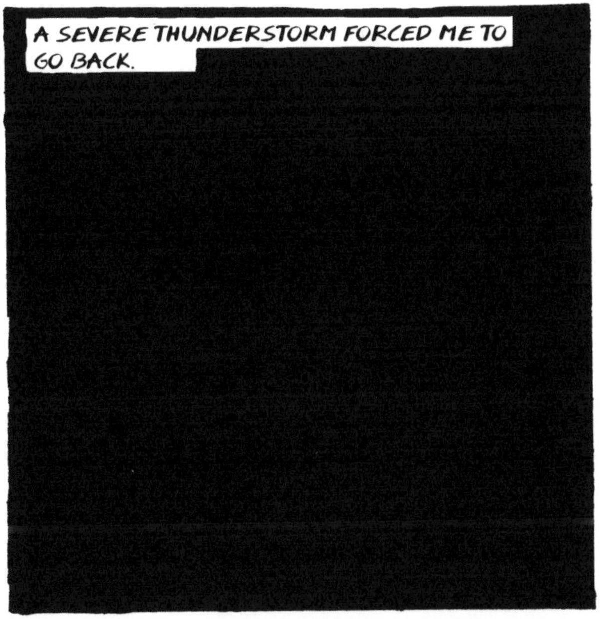
A SEVERE THUNDERSTORM FORCED ME TO GO BACK.

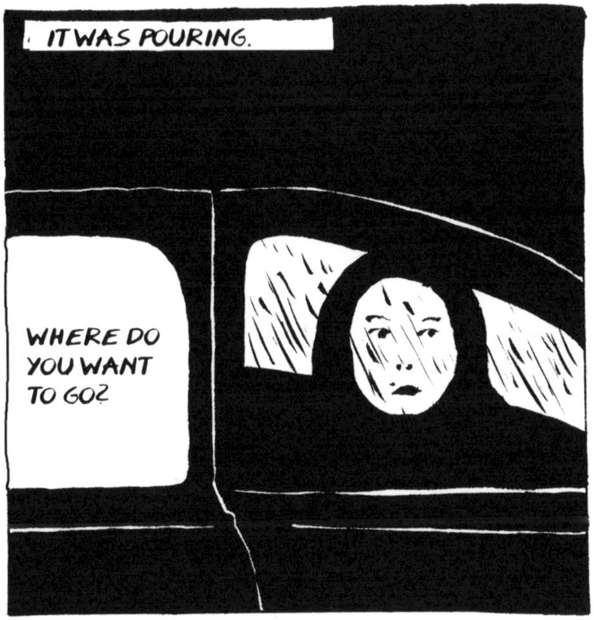
IT WAS POURING.
WHERE DO YOU WANT TO GO?

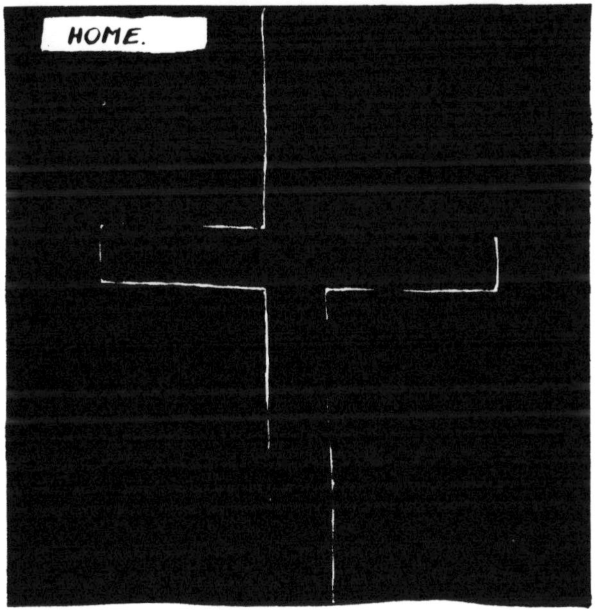
HOME.

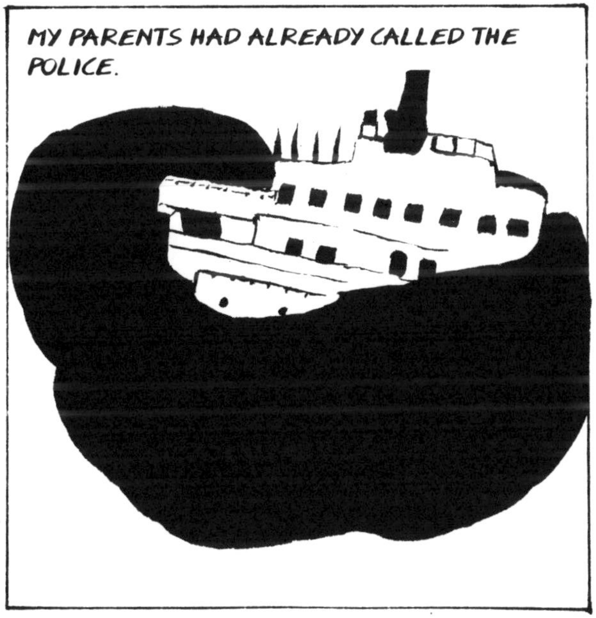
MY PARENTS HAD ALREADY CALLED THE POLICE.

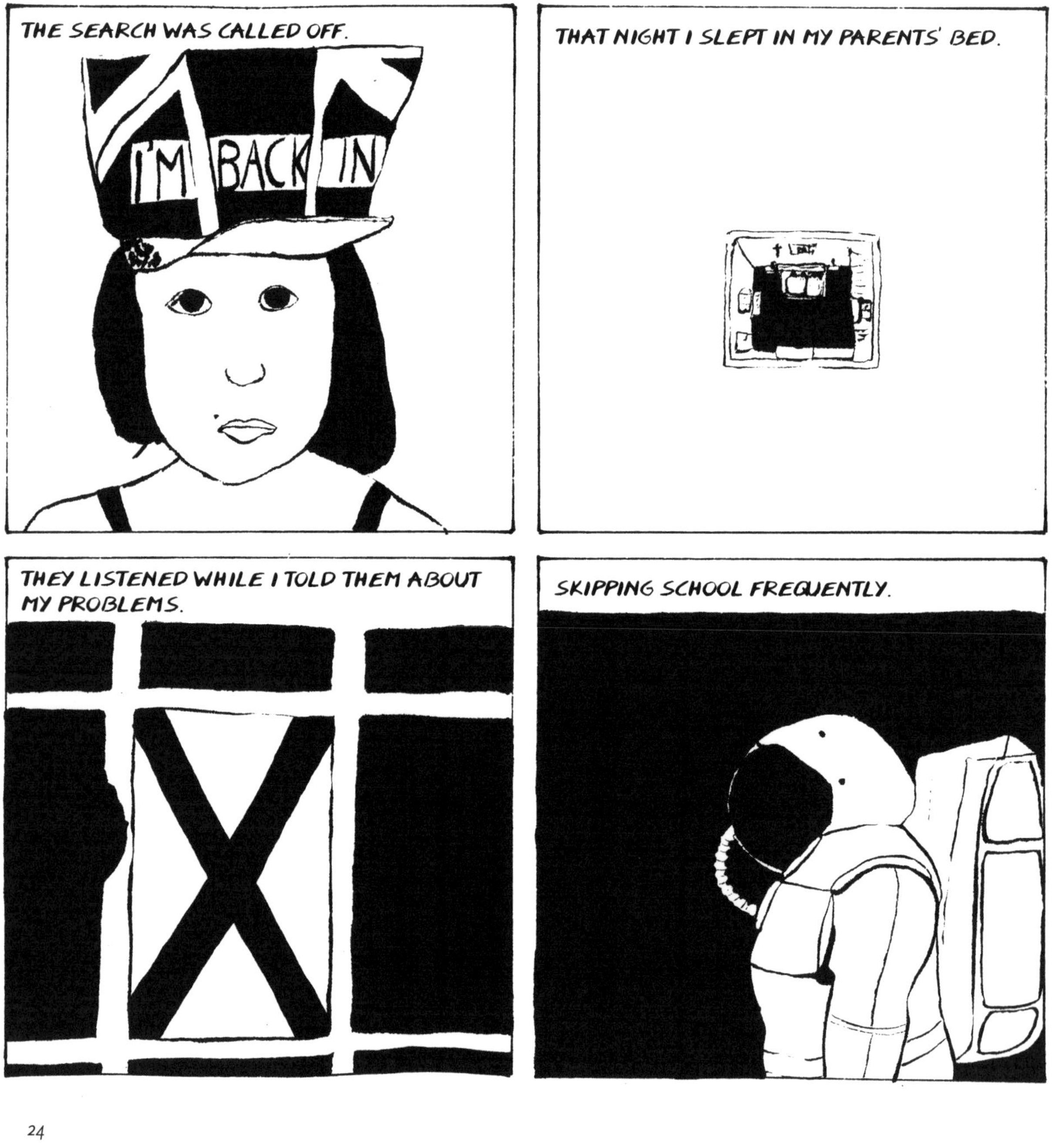
THE SEARCH WAS CALLED OFF.
I'M BACK IN
THAT NIGHT I SLEPT IN MY PARENTS' BED.
THEY LISTENED WHILE I TOLD THEM ABOUT MY PROBLEMS.
SKIPPING SCHOOL FREQUENTLY.

FLUNKING MATH.

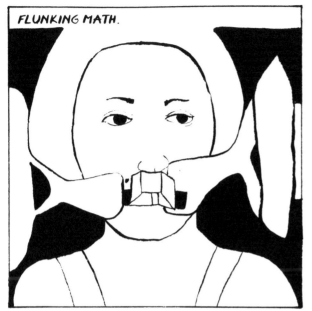

BUT I DID NOT MENTION MY BINGEING.

1 kg apples
leftover lunch
4 rolls (sausage + cheese)
1 pot of coffee
1 large chocolate bar
1 liter ice cream (family size)
leftover snacks
5 yogurts (250 g each)
5 slices of bread
1 bag of chips

FOR PEOPLE WHO DON'T HAVE AN EATING DISORDER, IT'S PERFECTLY NORMAL TO EAT WHEN YOU'RE HUNGRY WHENEVER POSSIBLE.

I WAS LIKE THAT FOR FIFTEEN YEARS.

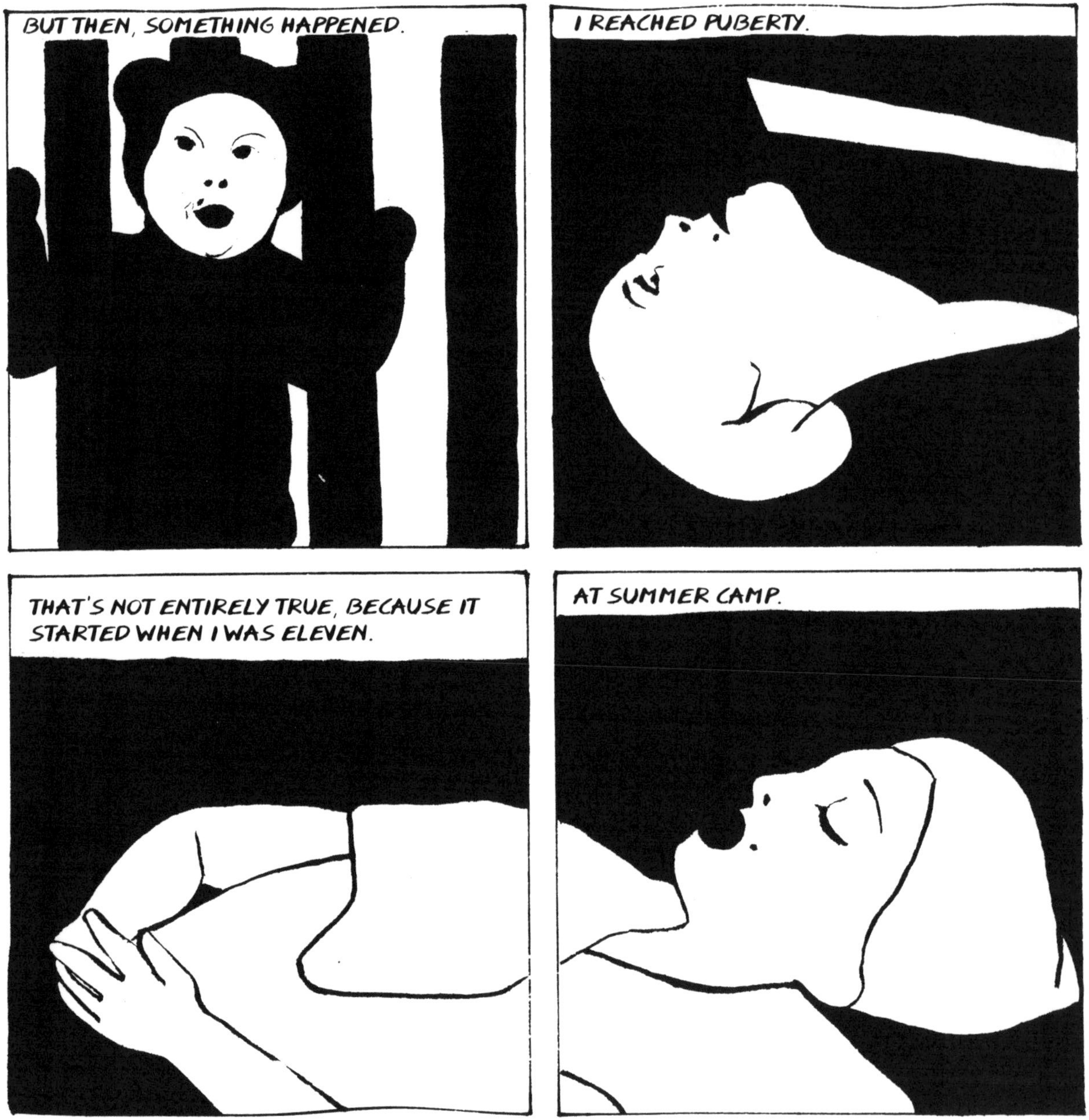
BUT THEN, SOMETHING HAPPENED.
I REACHED PUBERTY.
THAT'S NOT ENTIRELY TRUE, BECAUSE IT STARTED WHEN I WAS ELEVEN.
AT SUMMER CAMP.

I THOUGHT I HAD SOILED MY PANTS. NUMBER TWO.

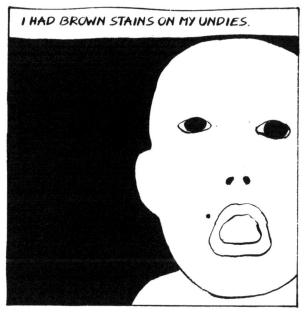

I HAD BROWN STAINS ON MY UNDIES.

I KEPT GETTING NAUSEATED TOO.

I THREW THOSE UNDIES OUT.

AND ONE DAY, WHEN I WAS SUPPOSED TO GO TO SWIM CLASS AT SCHOOL, IT HAPPENED AGAIN.

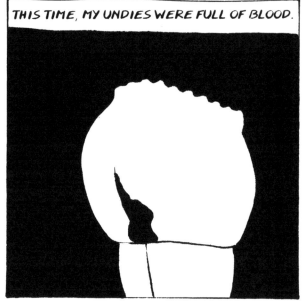

THIS TIME, MY UNDIES WERE FULL OF BLOOD.

SWIMMING WASN'T AN OPTION, AND I GOT MY GIRLFRIENDS TO PROMISE NOT TO TELL ANYONE.

BUT BECOMING A WOMAN COULD NOT BE STOPPED.

MY BREASTS STARTED GROWING WHEN I WAS NINE.

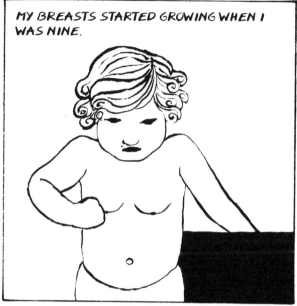

MY PUBIC HAIR GREW EVEN EARLIER.

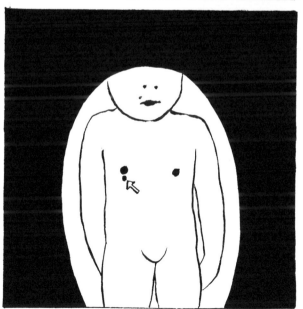

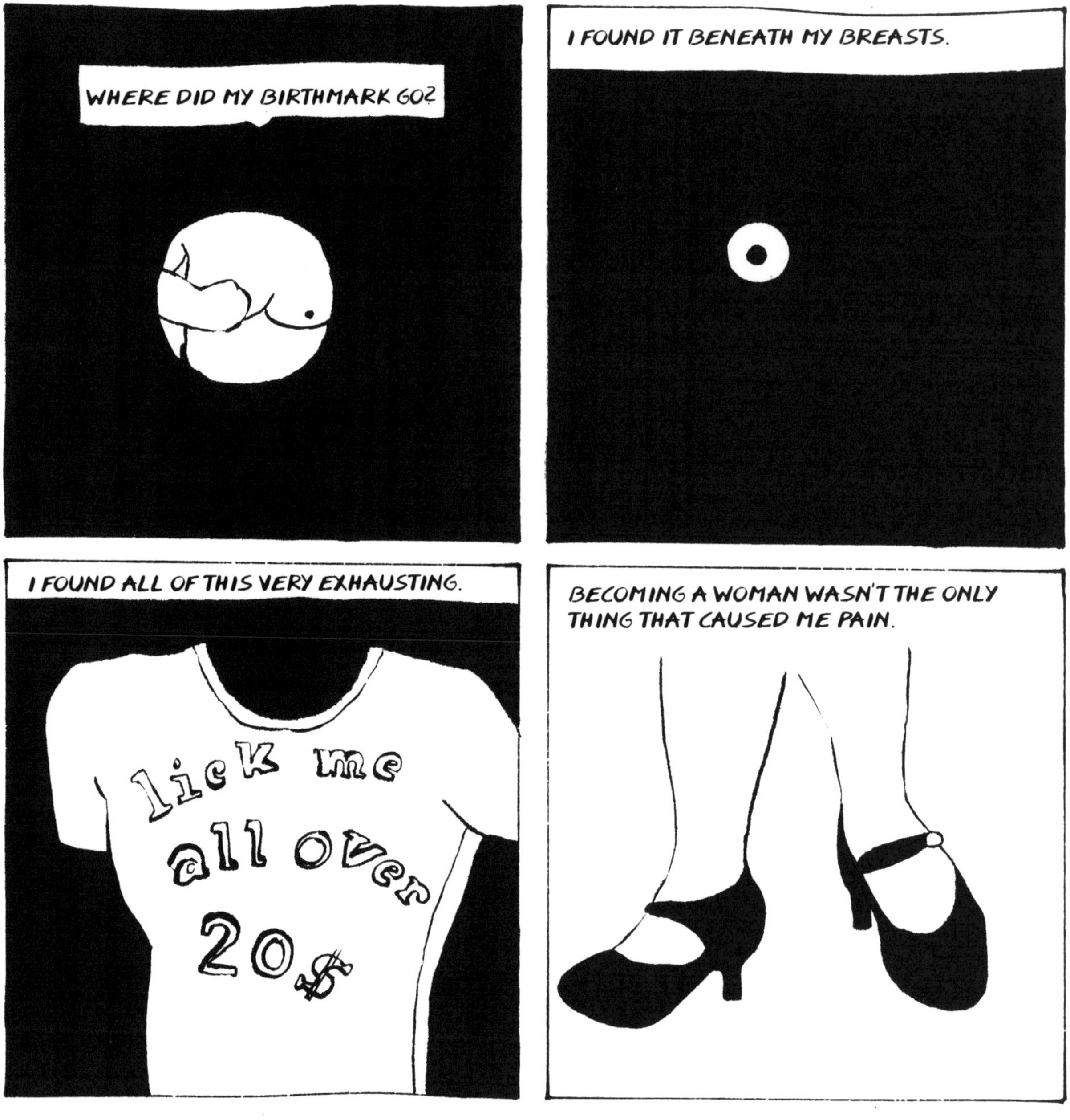
WHERE DID MY BIRTHMARK GO?
I FOUND IT BENEATH MY BREASTS.
I FOUND ALL OF THIS VERY EXHAUSTING.
lick me all over 20$
BECOMING A WOMAN WASN'T THE ONLY THING THAT CAUSED ME PAIN.

GROWING DID, TOO.

BECAUSE, ONCE AGAIN, IT WAS ALL HAPPENING TOO FAST.

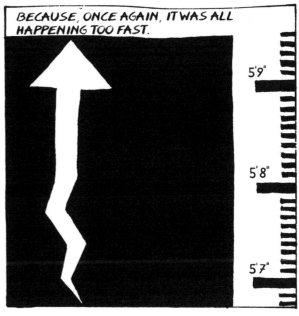

WITHIN JUST A COUPLE OF MONTHS I GREW ALMOST SIX INCHES.

MY KNEES HURT TERRIBLY, AND THE SKIN ON THEM STARTED TO CRACK.

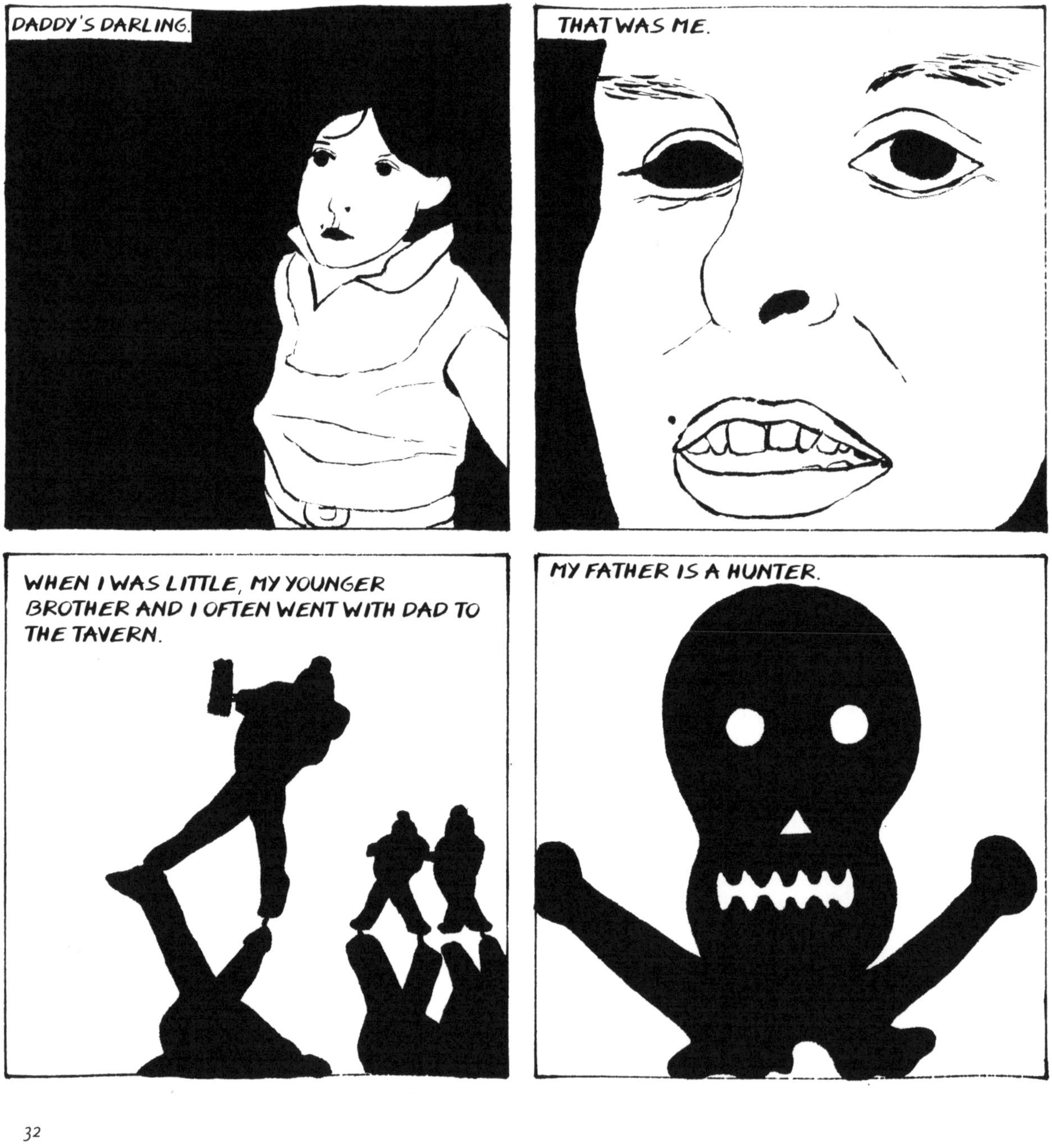
DADDY'S DARLING.
THAT WAS ME.
WHEN I WAS LITTLE, MY YOUNGER BROTHER AND I OFTEN WENT WITH DAD TO THE TAVERN.
MY FATHER IS A HUNTER.

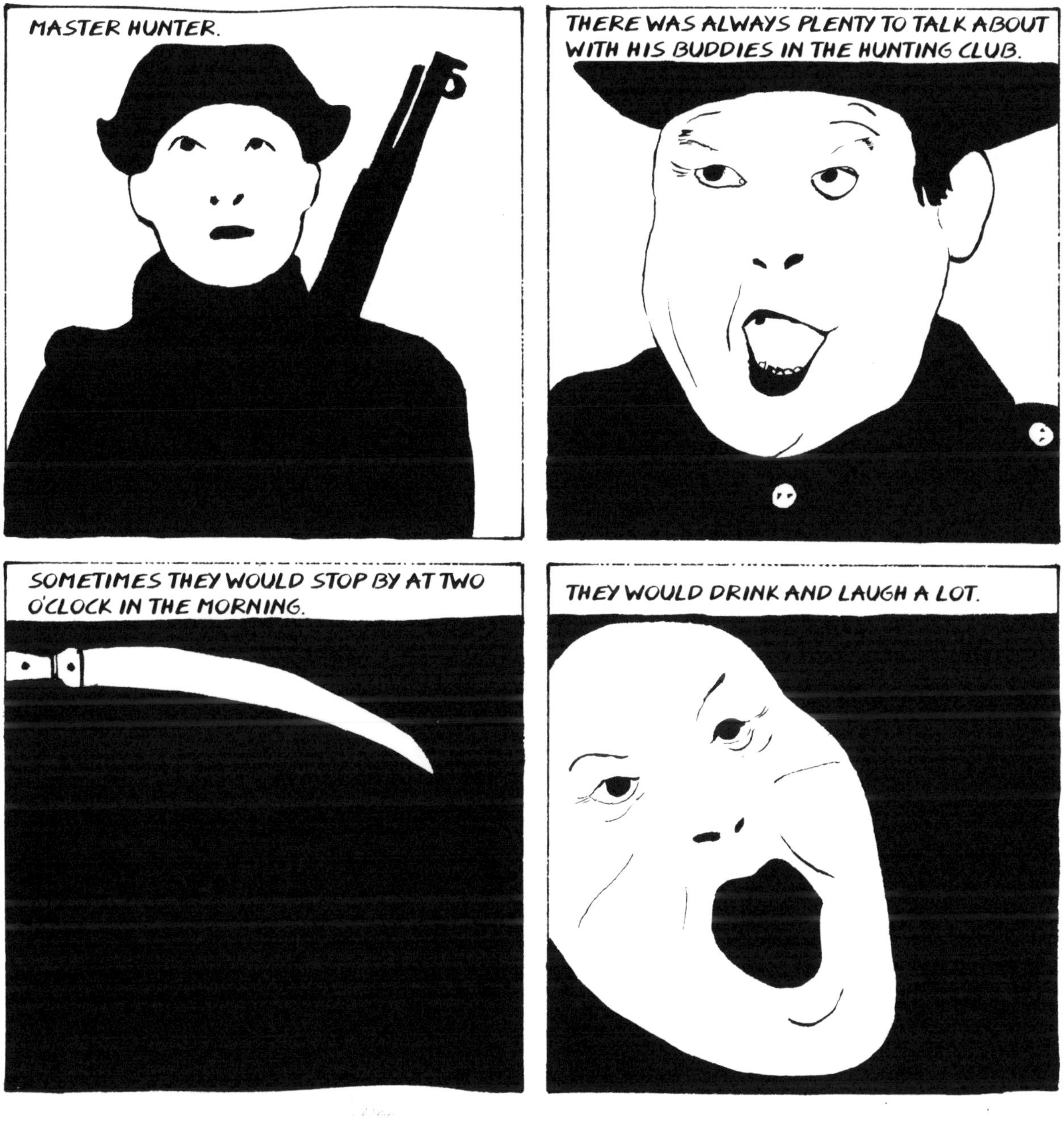
MASTER HUNTER.
THERE WAS ALWAYS PLENTY TO TALK ABOUT WITH HIS BUDDIES IN THE HUNTING CLUB.
SOMETIMES THEY WOULD STOP BY AT TWO O'CLOCK IN THE MORNING.
THEY WOULD DRINK AND LAUGH A LOT.

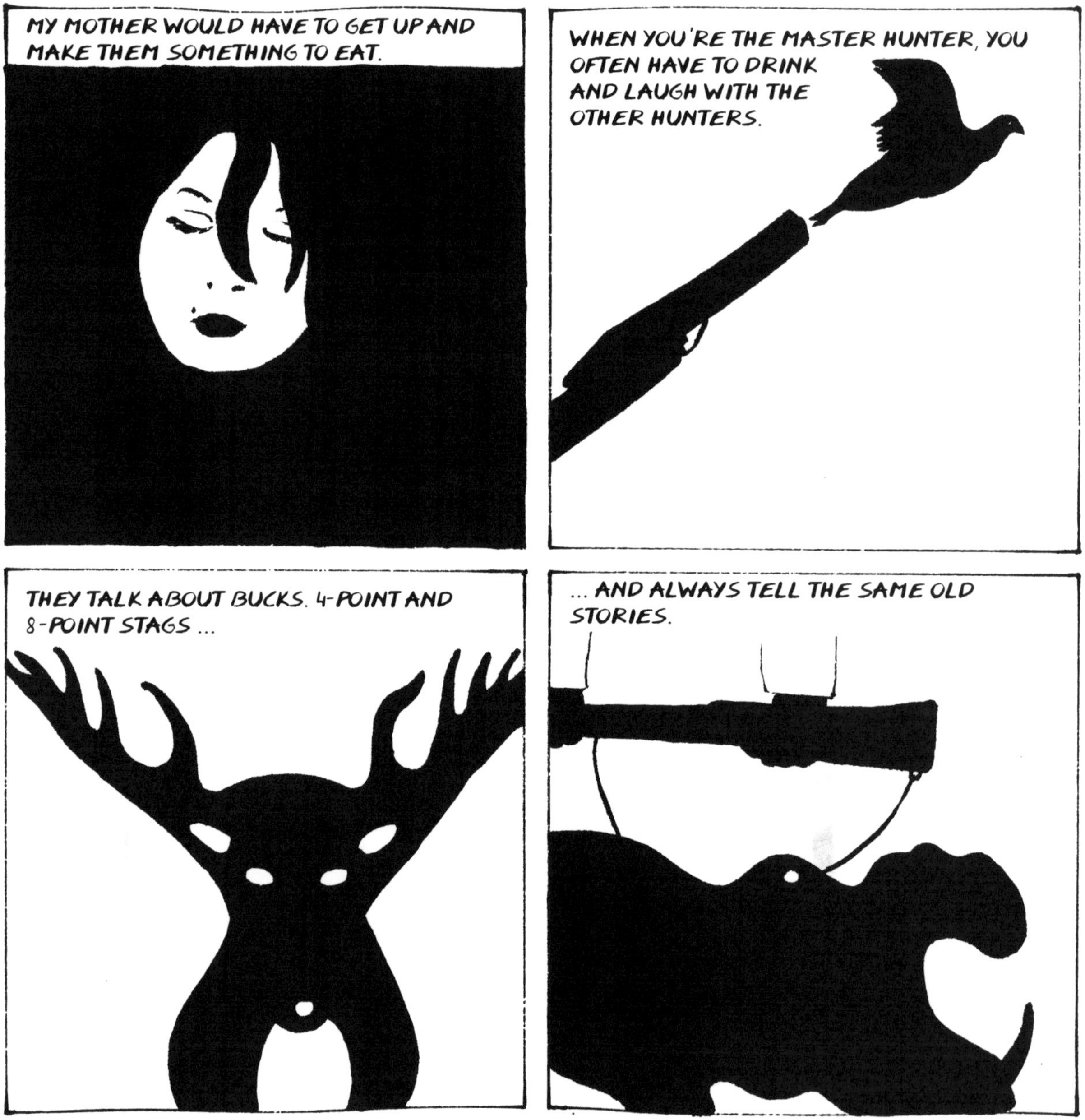
MY MOTHER WOULD HAVE TO GET UP AND MAKE THEM SOMETHING TO EAT.
WHEN YOU'RE THE MASTER HUNTER, YOU OFTEN HAVE TO DRINK AND LAUGH WITH THE OTHER HUNTERS.
THEY TALK ABOUT BUCKS. 4-POINT AND 8-POINT STAGS ...
... AND ALWAYS TELL THE SAME OLD STORIES.

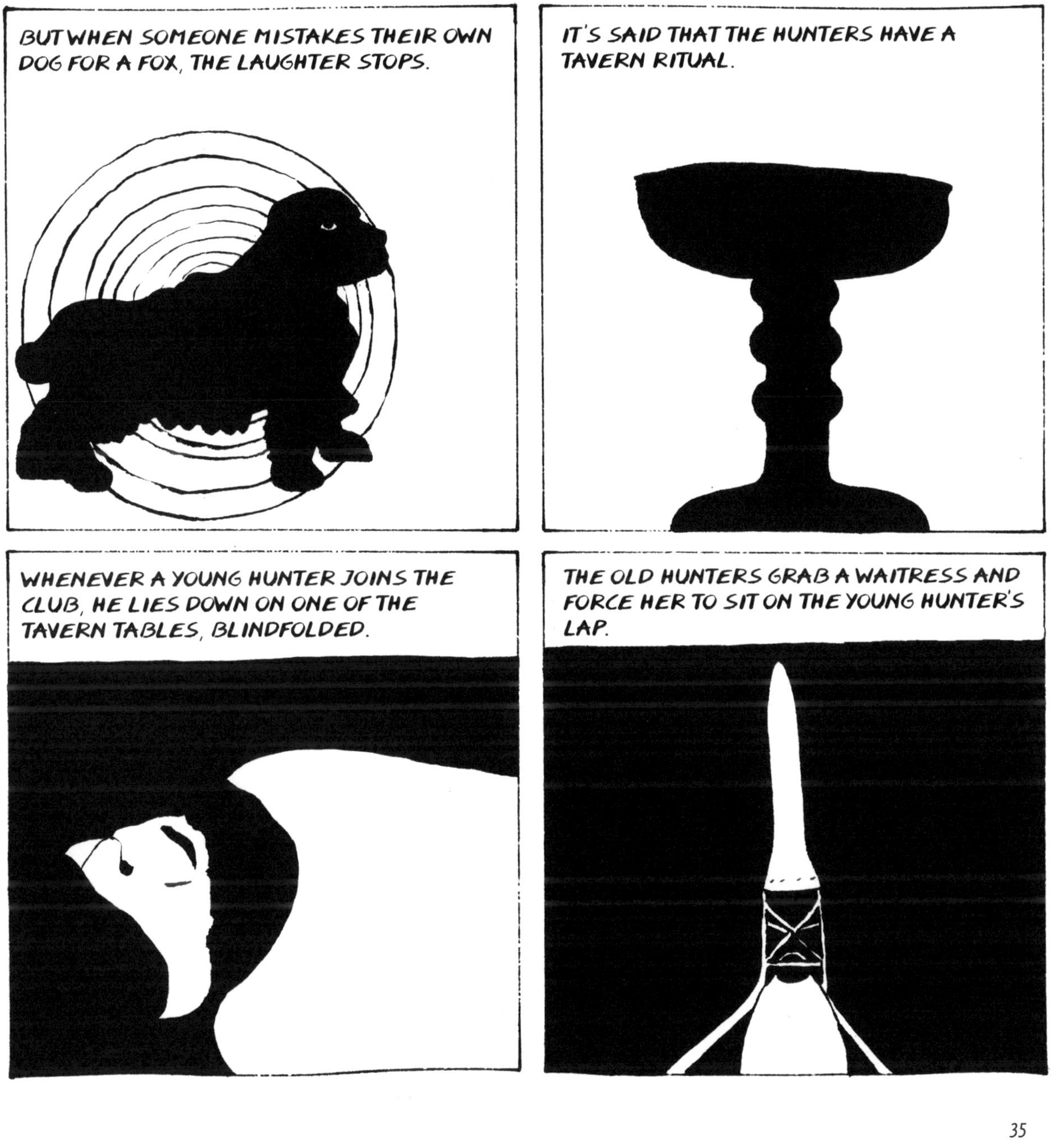
BUT WHEN SOMEONE MISTAKES THEIR OWN DOG FOR A FOX, THE LAUGHTER STOPS.
IT'S SAID THAT THE HUNTERS HAVE A TAVERN RITUAL.
WHENEVER A YOUNG HUNTER JOINS THE CLUB, HE LIES DOWN ON ONE OF THE TAVERN TABLES, BLINDFOLDED.
THE OLD HUNTERS GRAB A WAITRESS AND FORCE HER TO SIT ON THE YOUNG HUNTER'S LAP.

AFTERWARDS, THE MEN MAKE THRUSTING GESTURES AT THE WOMAN TO SYMBOLIZE SEXUAL INTERCOURSE.

BECOMING A MAN = BECOMING A HUNTER.

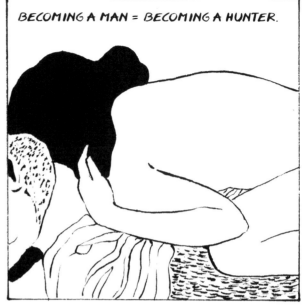

WHENEVER A HUNTER BAGGED AN ANIMAL, HE HAD TO SHOW IT TO MY FATHER, THE MASTER HUNTER.

I'VE SEEN A LOT OF DEAD DEER, BOARS, AND RABBITS.

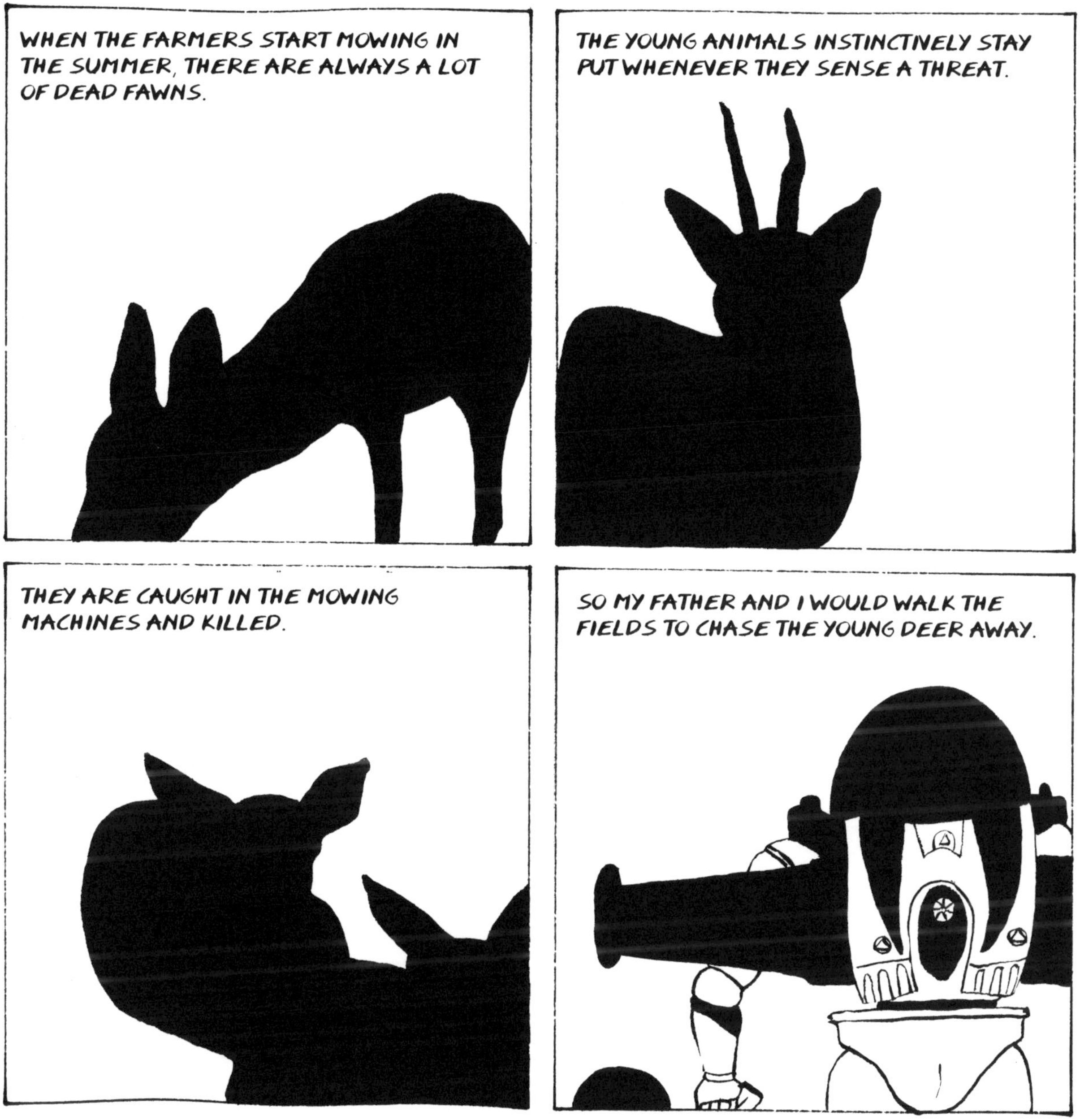
WHEN THE FARMERS START MOWING IN THE SUMMER, THERE ARE ALWAYS A LOT OF DEAD FAWNS.
THE YOUNG ANIMALS INSTINCTIVELY STAY PUT WHENEVER THEY SENSE A THREAT.
THEY ARE CAUGHT IN THE MOWING MACHINES AND KILLED.
SO MY FATHER AND I WOULD WALK THE FIELDS TO CHASE THE YOUNG DEER AWAY.

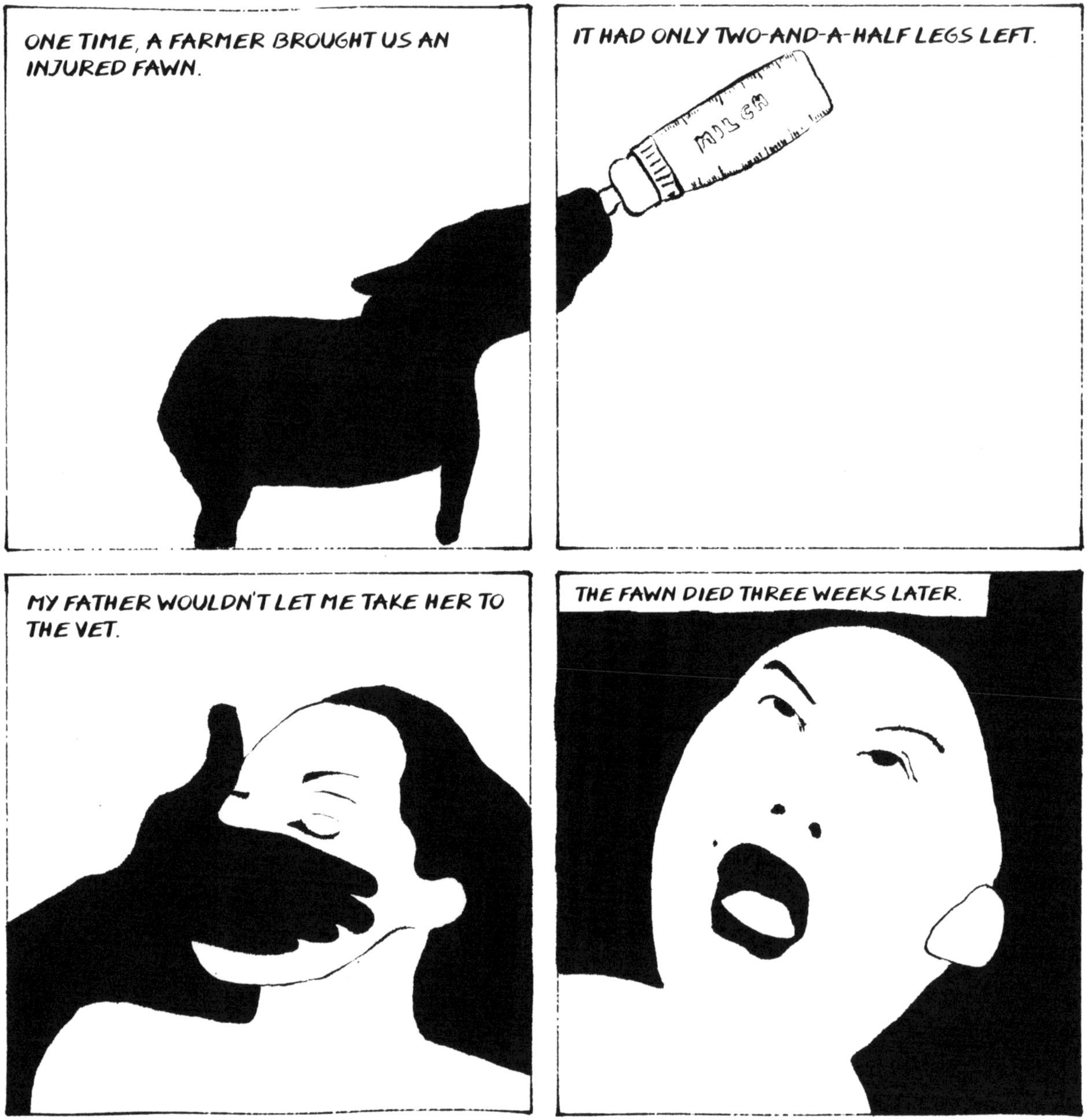
ONE TIME, A FARMER BROUGHT US AN INJURED FAWN.
IT HAD ONLY TWO-AND-A-HALF LEGS LEFT.
MY FATHER WOULDN'T LET ME TAKE HER TO THE VET.
THE FAWN DIED THREE WEEKS LATER.

I WAS OFTEN ANGRY AT MY FATHER.

MY FATHER SMOKED FOUR PACKS OF CIGARETTES A DAY.

SEVEN CIGARETTES AT BREAKFAST.

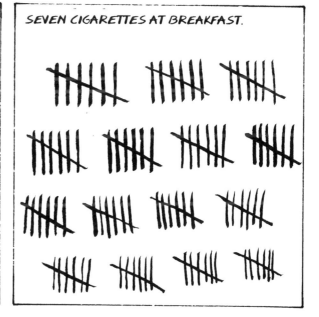

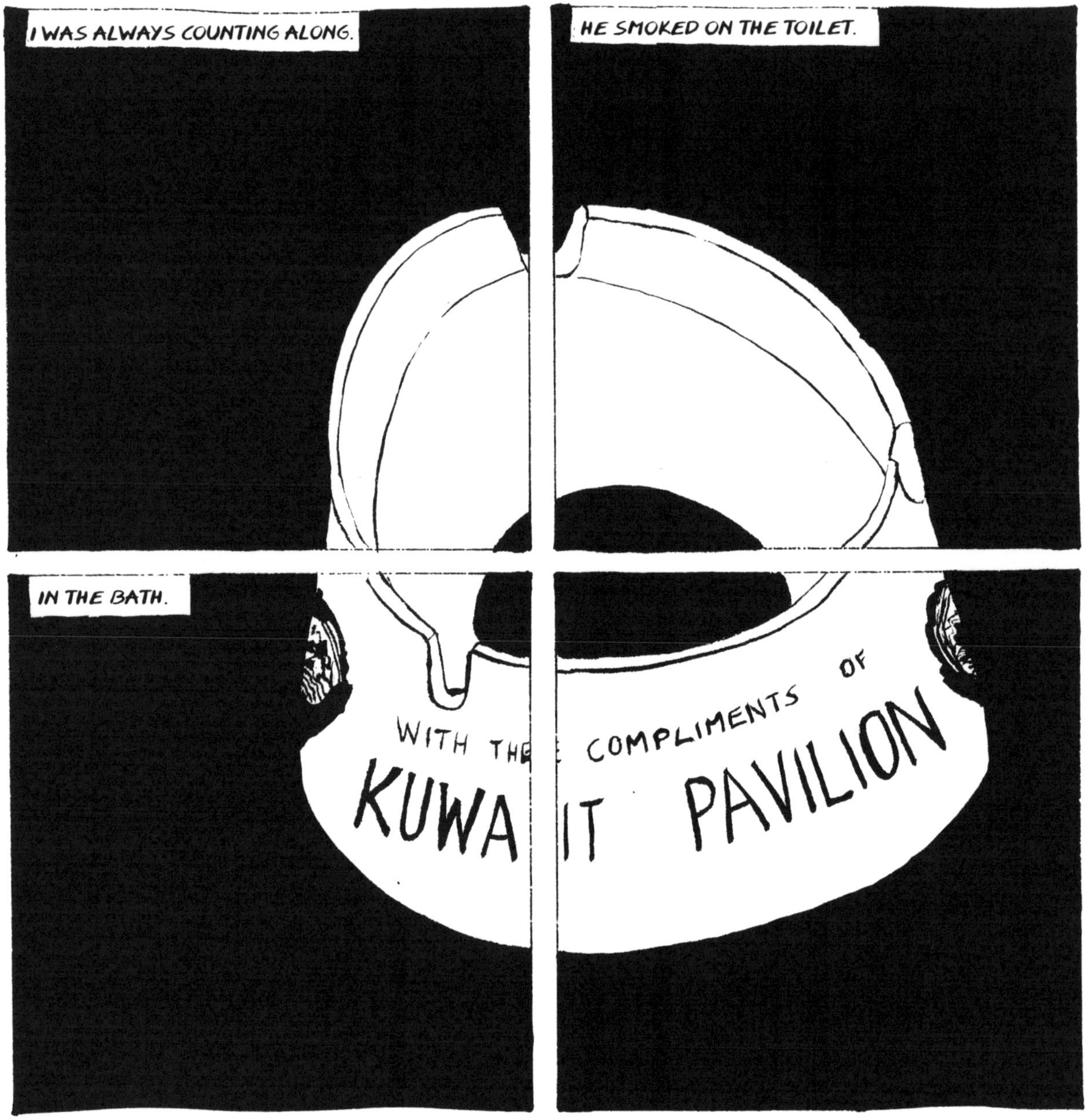
I WAS ALWAYS COUNTING ALONG.
HE SMOKED ON THE TOILET.
IN THE BATH.
WITH THE COMPLIMENTS OF
KUWAIT PAVILION

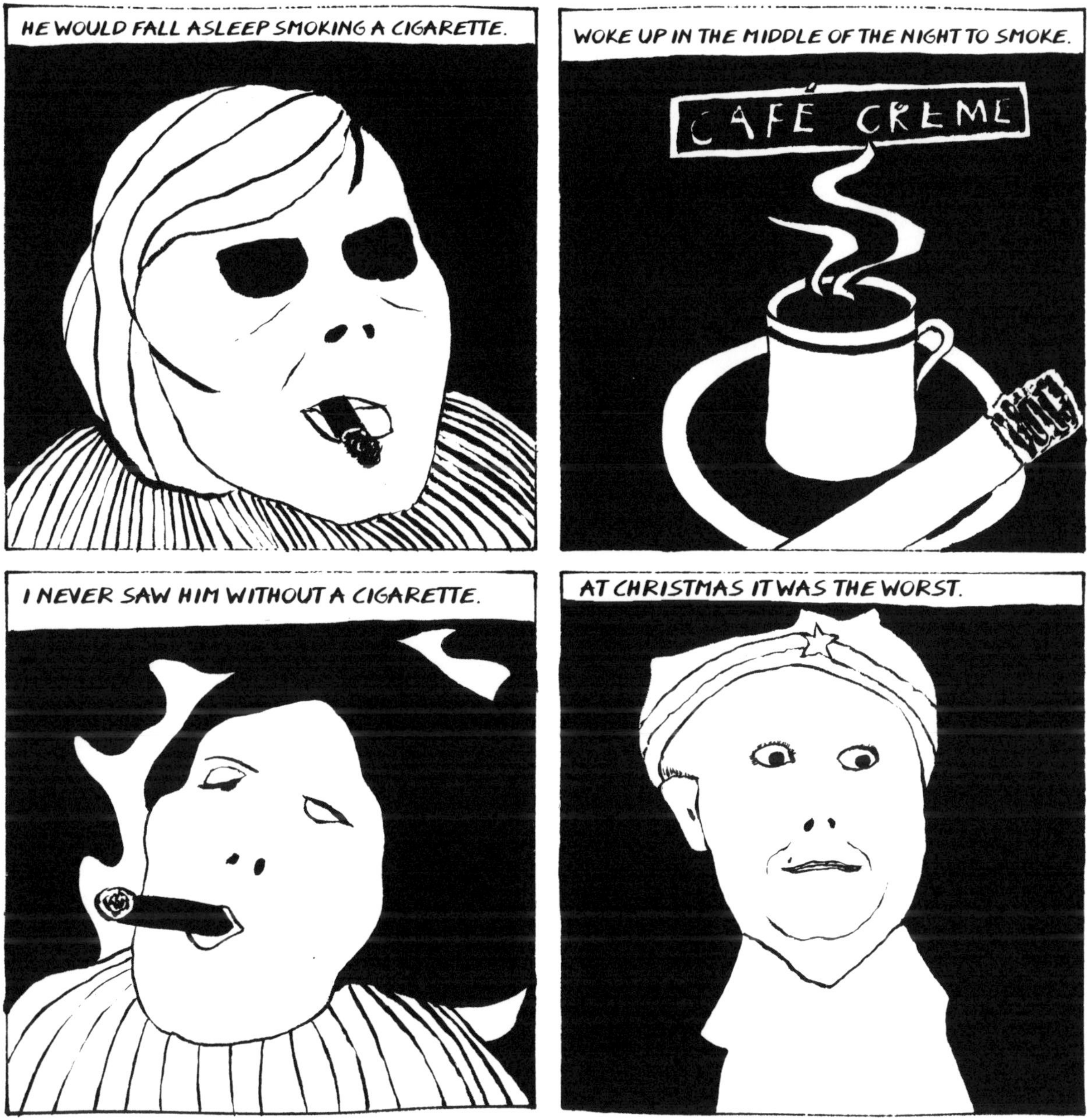
HE WOULD FALL ASLEEP SMOKING A CIGARETTE.
WOKE UP IN THE MIDDLE OF THE NIGHT TO SMOKE.
CAFÉ CREME
I NEVER SAW HIM WITHOUT A CIGARETTE.
AT CHRISTMAS IT WAS THE WORST.

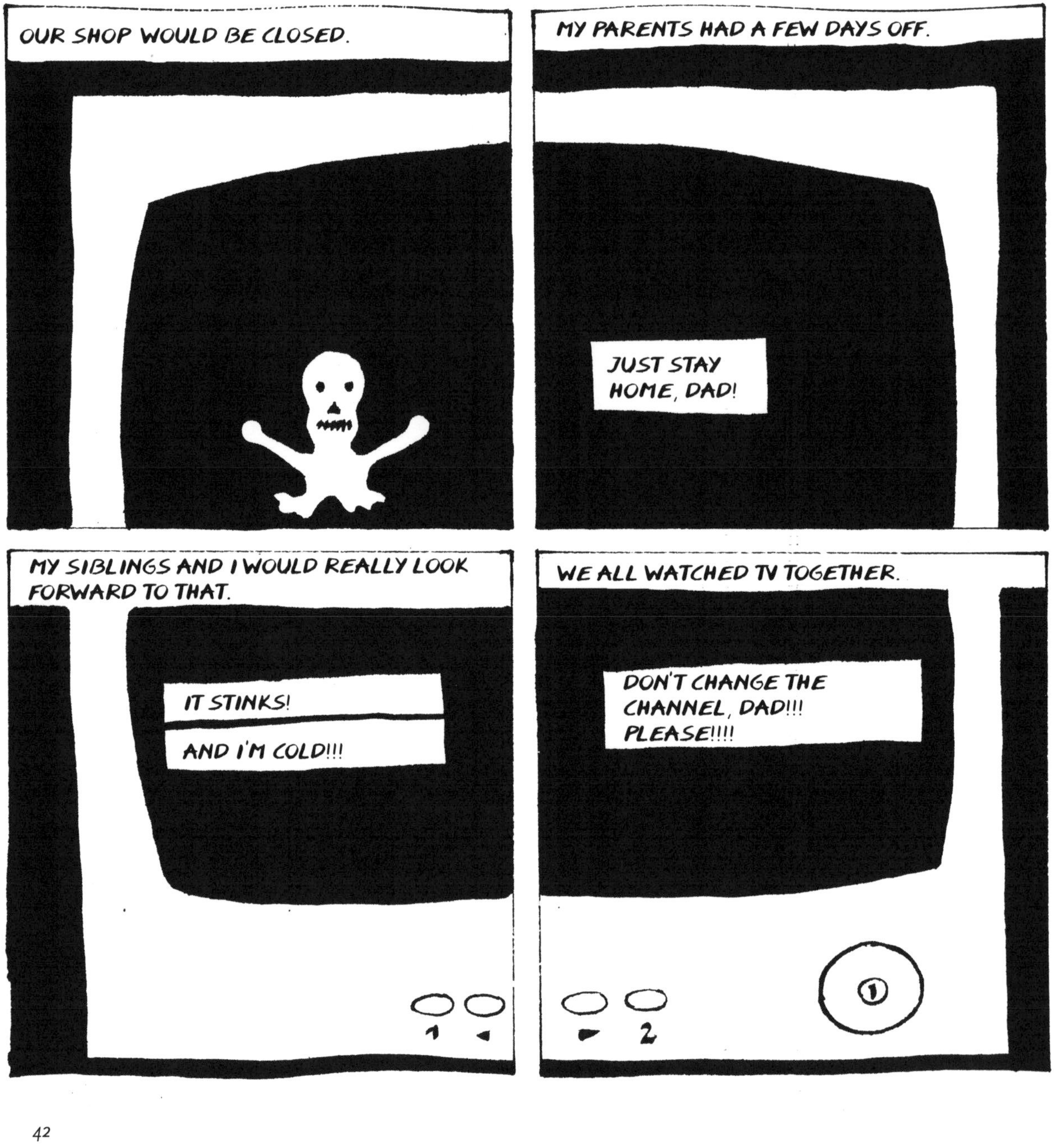
OUR SHOP WOULD BE CLOSED.
MY PARENTS HAD A FEW DAYS OFF.
JUST STAY HOME, DAD!
MY SIBLINGS AND I WOULD REALLY LOOK FORWARD TO THAT.
IT STINKS!
AND I'M COLD!!!
WE ALL WATCHED TV TOGETHER.
DON'T CHANGE THE CHANNEL, DAD!!! PLEASE!!!!

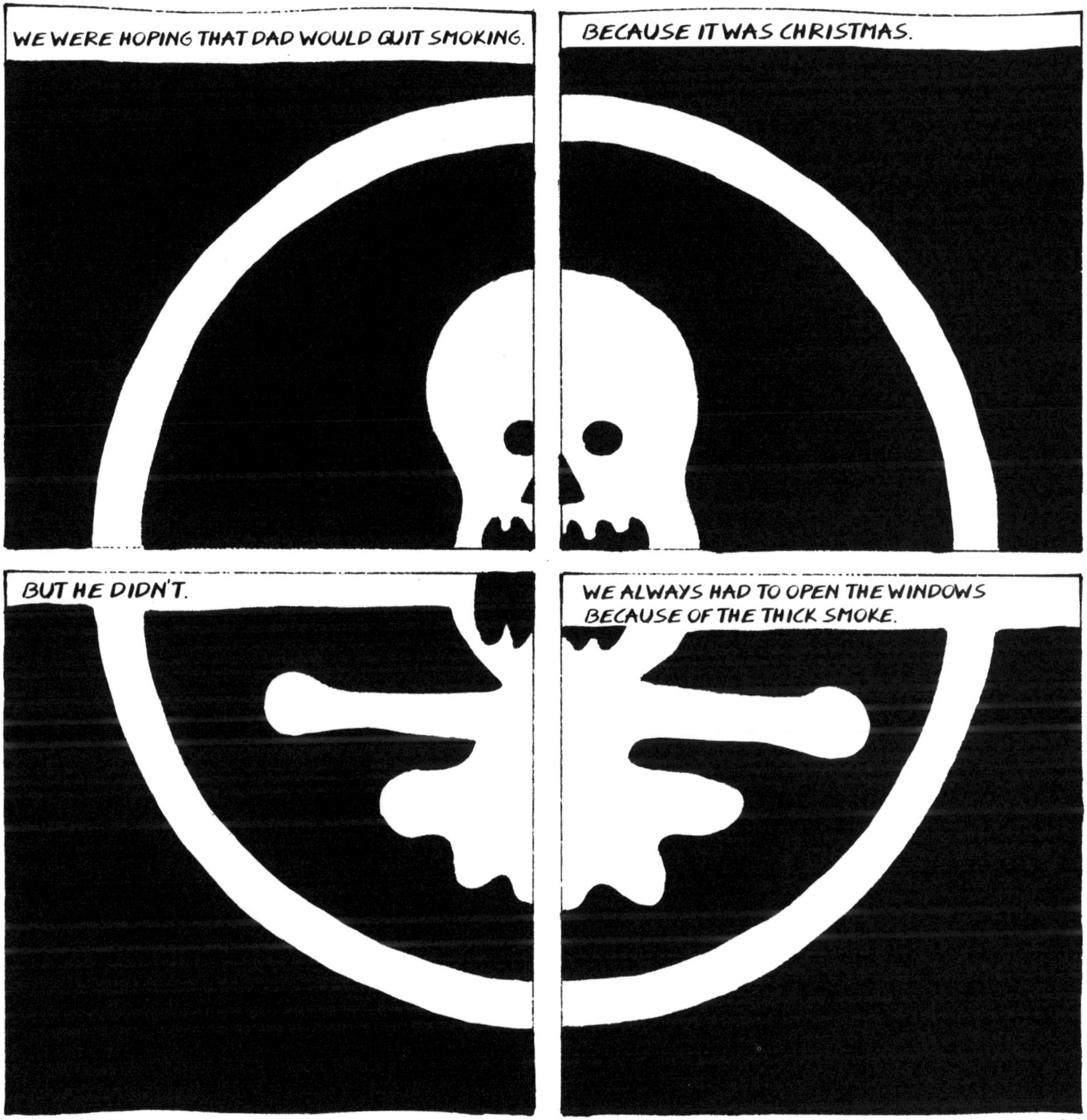
WE WERE HOPING THAT DAD WOULD QUIT SMOKING.
BECAUSE IT WAS CHRISTMAS.
BUT HE DIDN'T.
WE ALWAYS HAD TO OPEN THE WINDOWS BECAUSE OF THE THICK SMOKE.

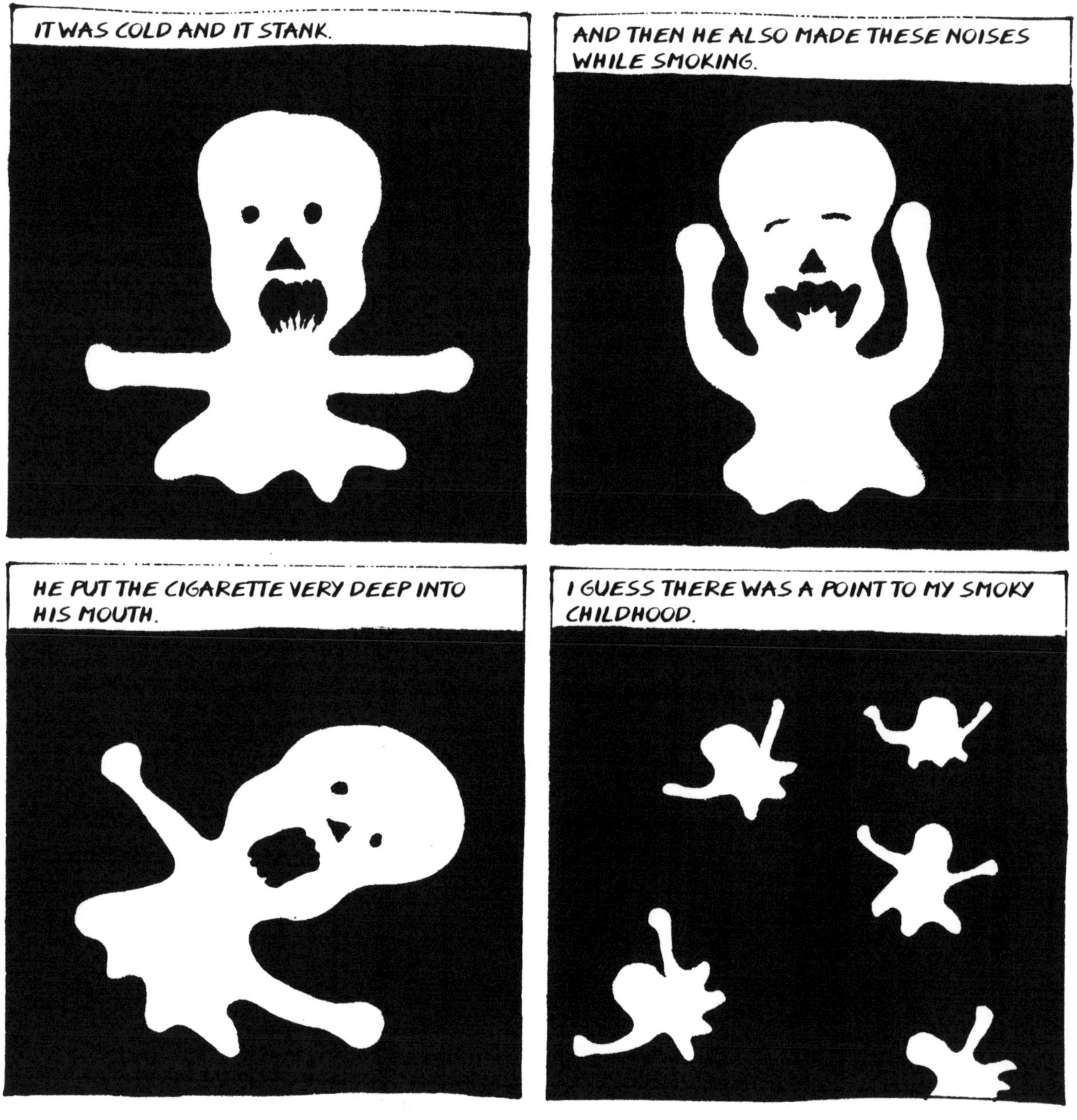
IT WAS COLD AND IT STANK.
AND THEN HE ALSO MADE THESE NOISES WHILE SMOKING.
HE PUT THE CIGARETTE VERY DEEP INTO HIS MOUTH.
I GUESS THERE WAS A POINT TO MY SMOKY CHILDHOOD.

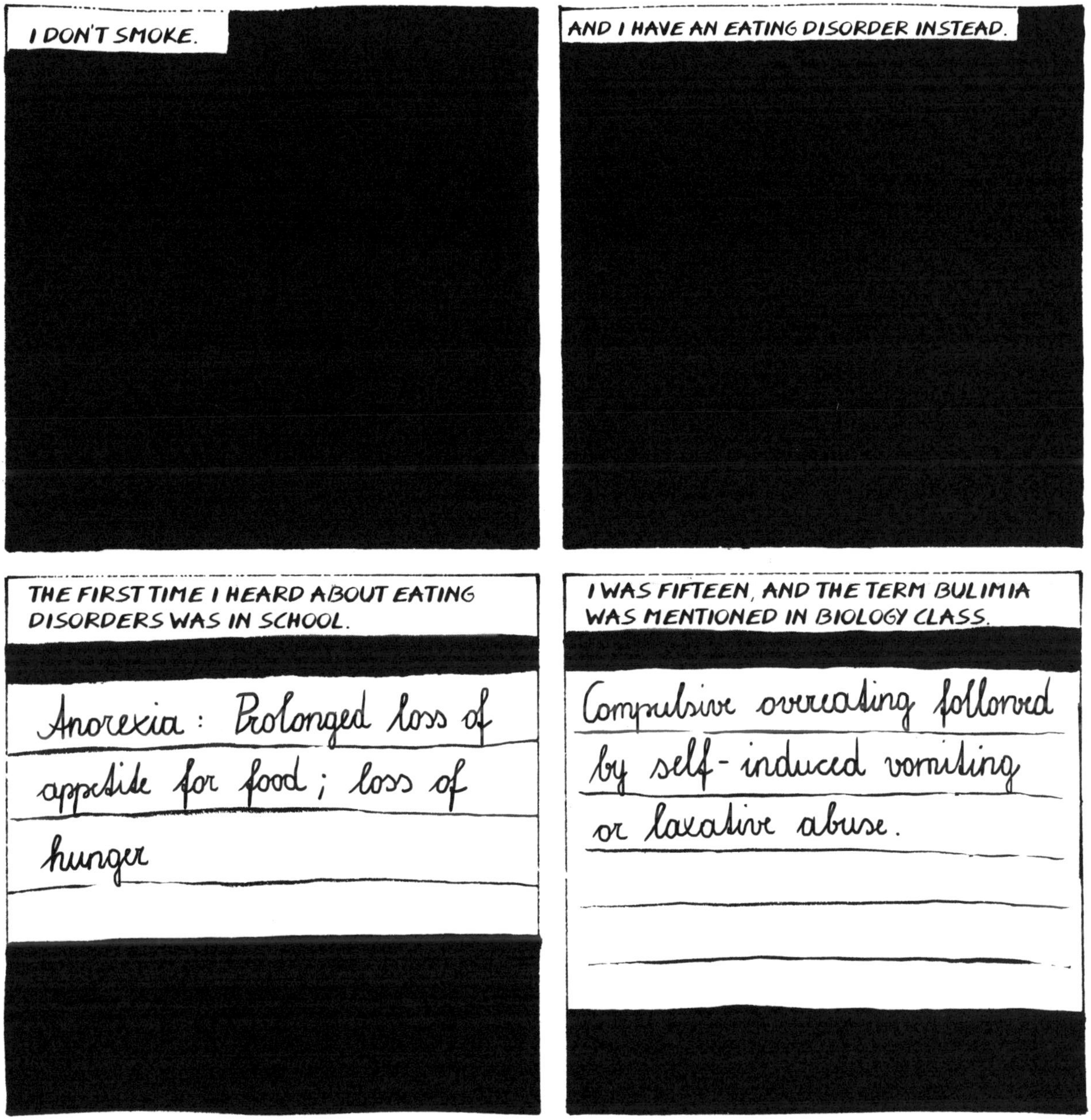
I DON'T SMOKE.
AND I HAVE AN EATING DISORDER INSTEAD.
THE FIRST TIME I HEARD ABOUT EATING DISORDERS WAS IN SCHOOL.
Anorexia: Prolonged loss of appetite for food; loss of hunger
I WAS FIFTEEN, AND THE TERM BULIMIA WAS MENTIONED IN BIOLOGY CLASS.
Compulsive overeating followed by self-induced vomiting or laxative abuse.

YOU EAT UNTIL YOU PUKE.

IF IT DOESN'T HAPPEN ON ITS OWN, YOU USE YOUR FINGER.

YOU STICK YOUR FINGER INTO THE BACK OF YOUR MOUTH AND TICKLE YOUR UVULA.

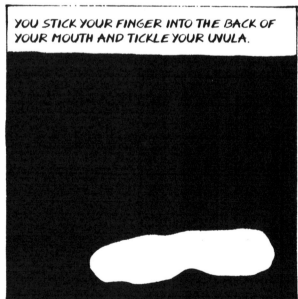

IT'S IMPORTANT TO EAT FOOD THAT COMES UP EASILY.

WHEN YOU EAT FOOD THAT DOESN'T, IT CAN HURT A LOT.

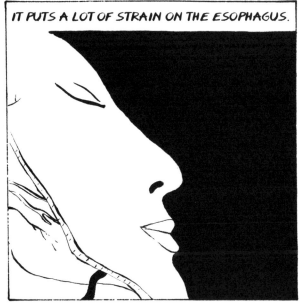

IT PUTS A LOT OF STRAIN ON THE ESOPHAGUS.

TO THE POINT WHERE YOU CAN EVEN TEAR YOUR ESOPHAGUS.

GOOD FOR PUKING ARE: NOODLES, TOAST, ICE CREAM, CHOCOLATE ...

... REALLY ANYTHING SOFT.

NOT SO GREAT ARE: FRUIT, RAW VEGETABLES, BROWN BREAD (CRUST) ...

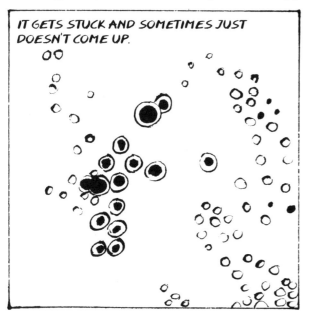

IT GETS STUCK AND SOMETIMES JUST DOESN'T COME UP.

CHEWING EVERYTHING WELL IS THE BEST RECIPE FOR EFFICIENT PUKING.

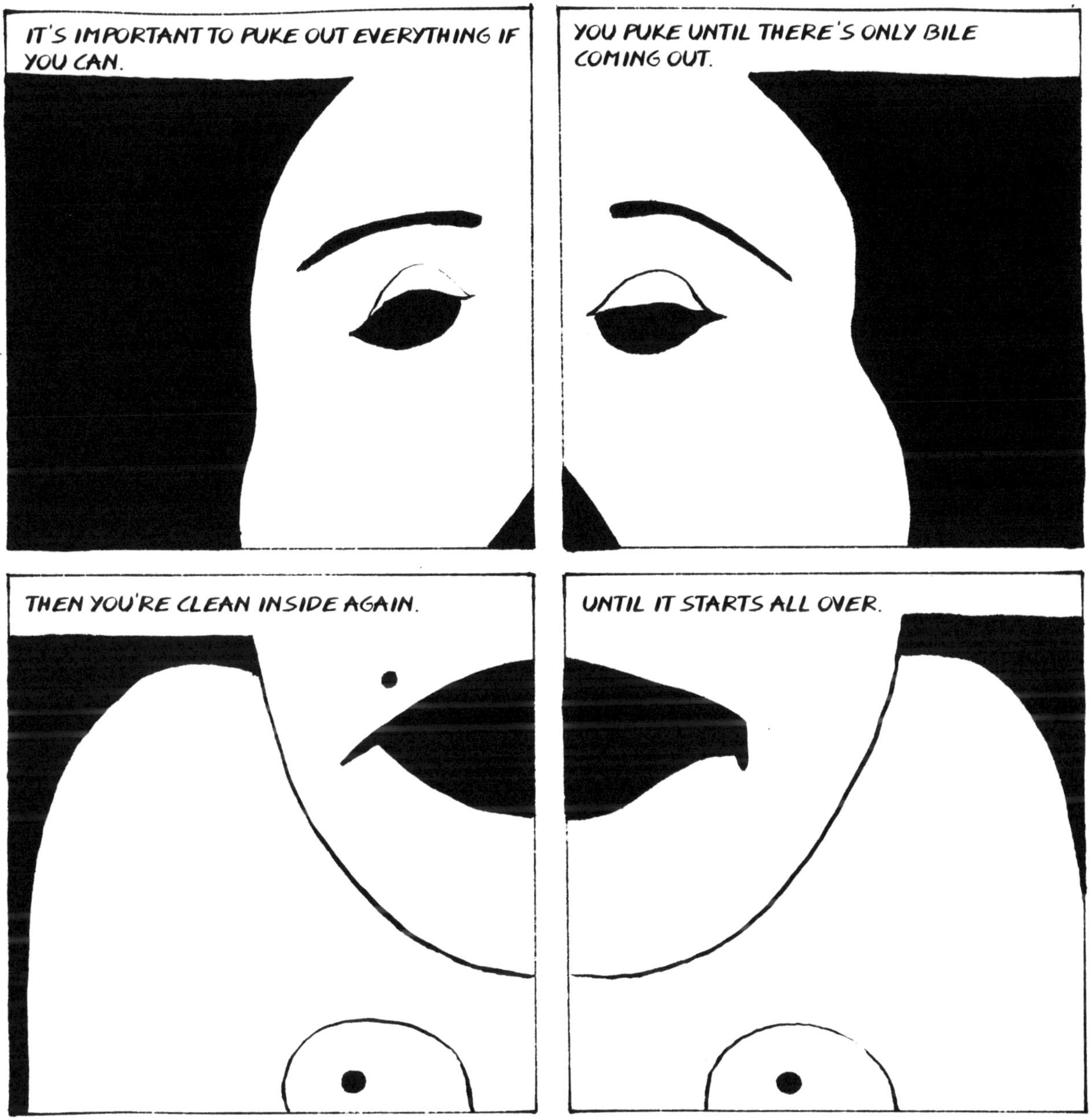
IT'S IMPORTANT TO PUKE OUT EVERYTHING IF YOU CAN.
YOU PUKE UNTIL THERE'S ONLY BILE COMING OUT.
THEN YOU'RE CLEAN INSIDE AGAIN.
UNTIL IT STARTS ALL OVER.

I DIDN'T PUKE WHEN I FIRST STARTED BINGEING.

SO I DIDN'T HAVE AN EATING DISORDER.

WHEN THE STOMACHACHE FROM GORGING BECAME UNBEARABLE,

I WOULD STICK A FINGER IN MY MOUTH.

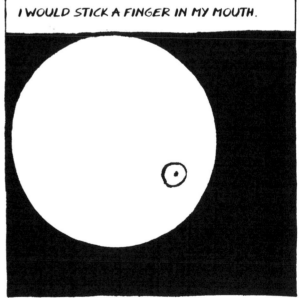

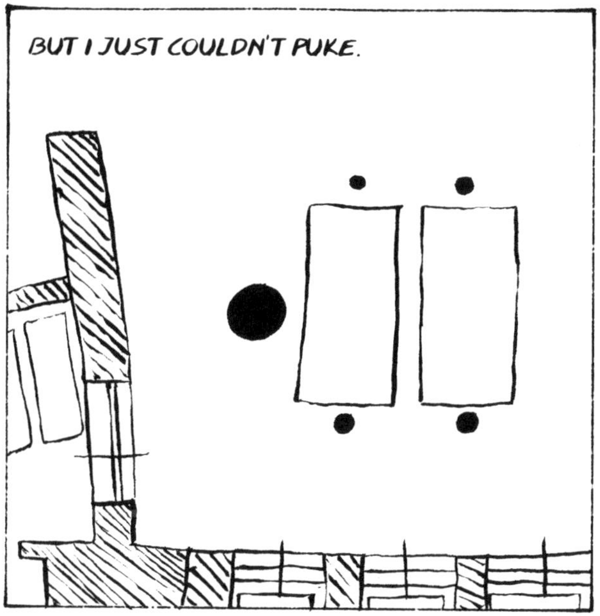
BUT I JUST COULDN'T PUKE.

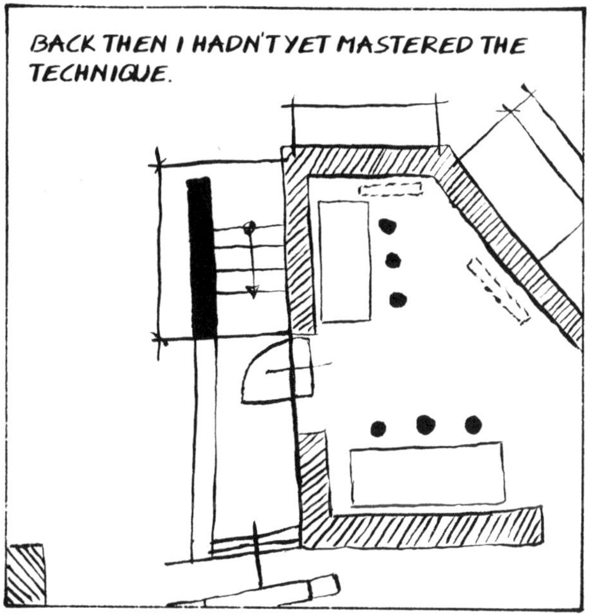
BACK THEN I HADN'T YET MASTERED THE TECHNIQUE.

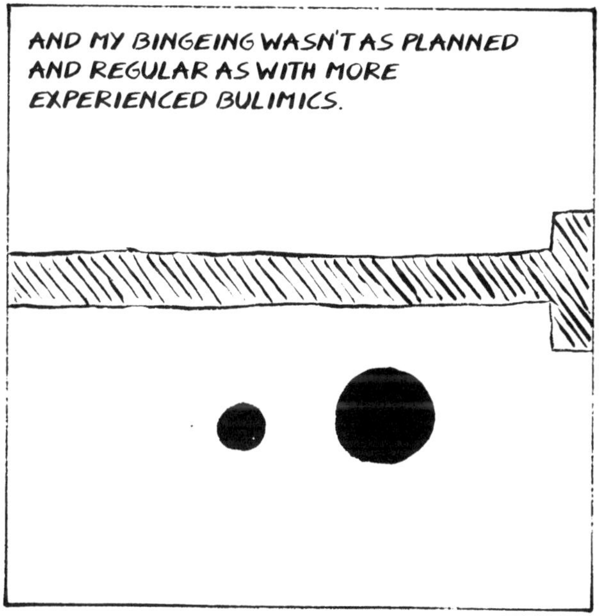
AND MY BINGEING WASN'T AS PLANNED AND REGULAR AS WITH MORE EXPERIENCED BULIMICS.

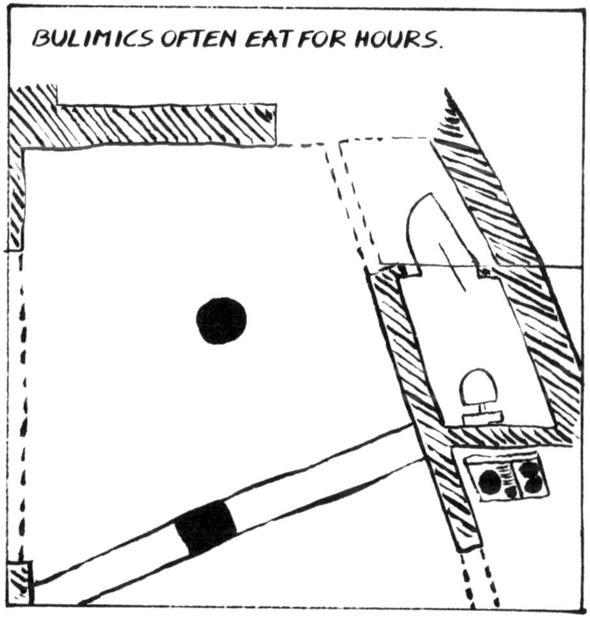
BULIMICS OFTEN EAT FOR HOURS.

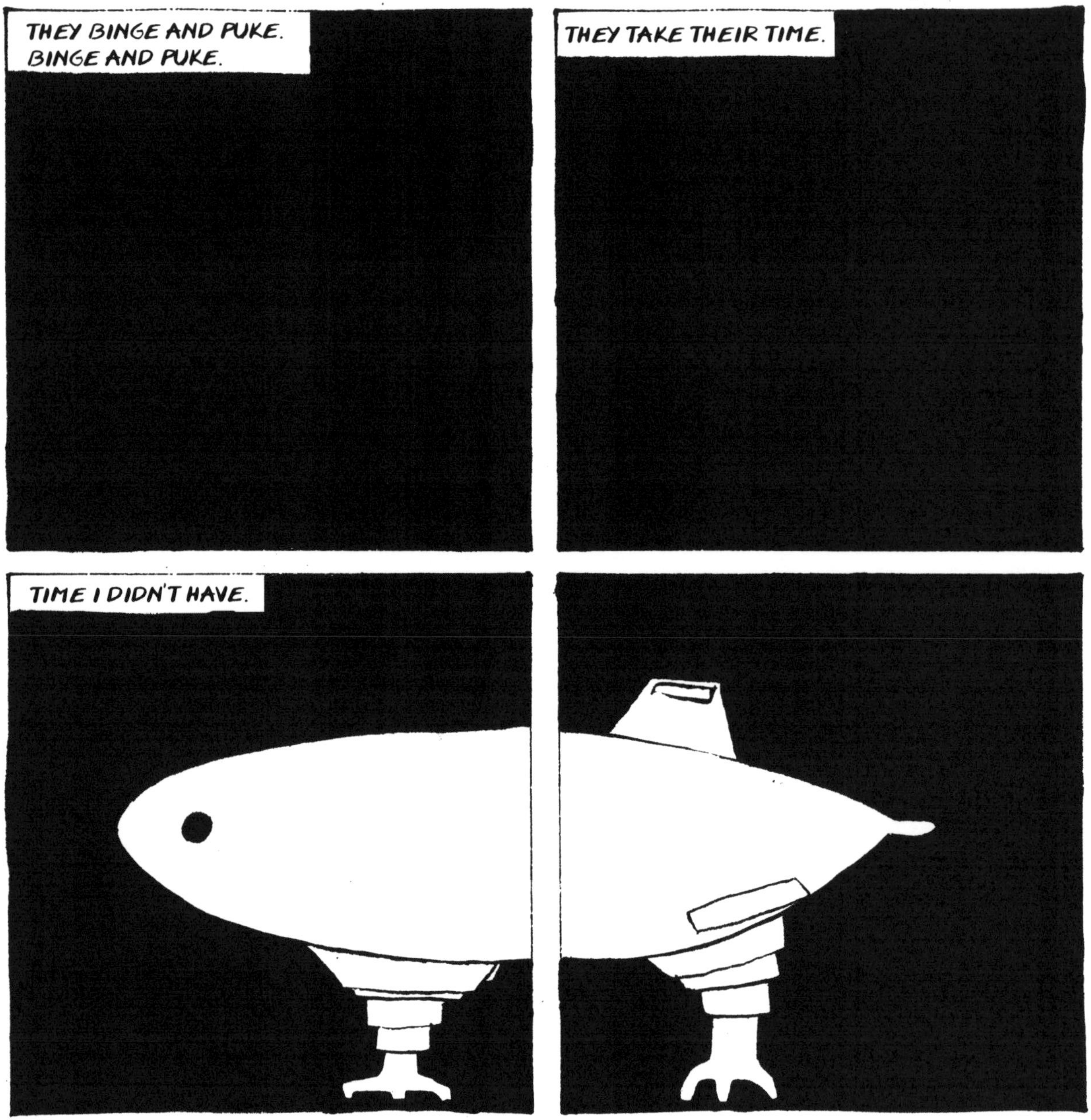
THEY BINGE AND PUKE. BINGE AND PUKE.
THEY TAKE THEIR TIME.
TIME I DIDN'T HAVE.

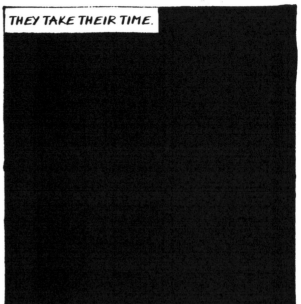

I HAD NO IDEA WHEN I WOULD BE AMBUSHED BY THE NEXT BINGE ATTACK.

I WOULD CRAM AS MUCH AS I COULD IN MY MOUTH, AS FAST AS I COULD.

UNTIL I COULDN'T TAKE ANY MORE.

MY STOMACH WOULD BULGE, AND I WOULD FALL ASLEEP, EXHAUSTED.

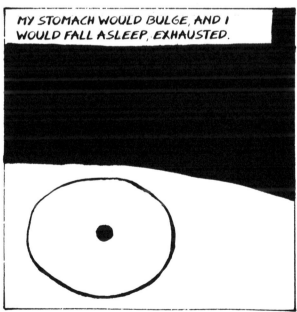

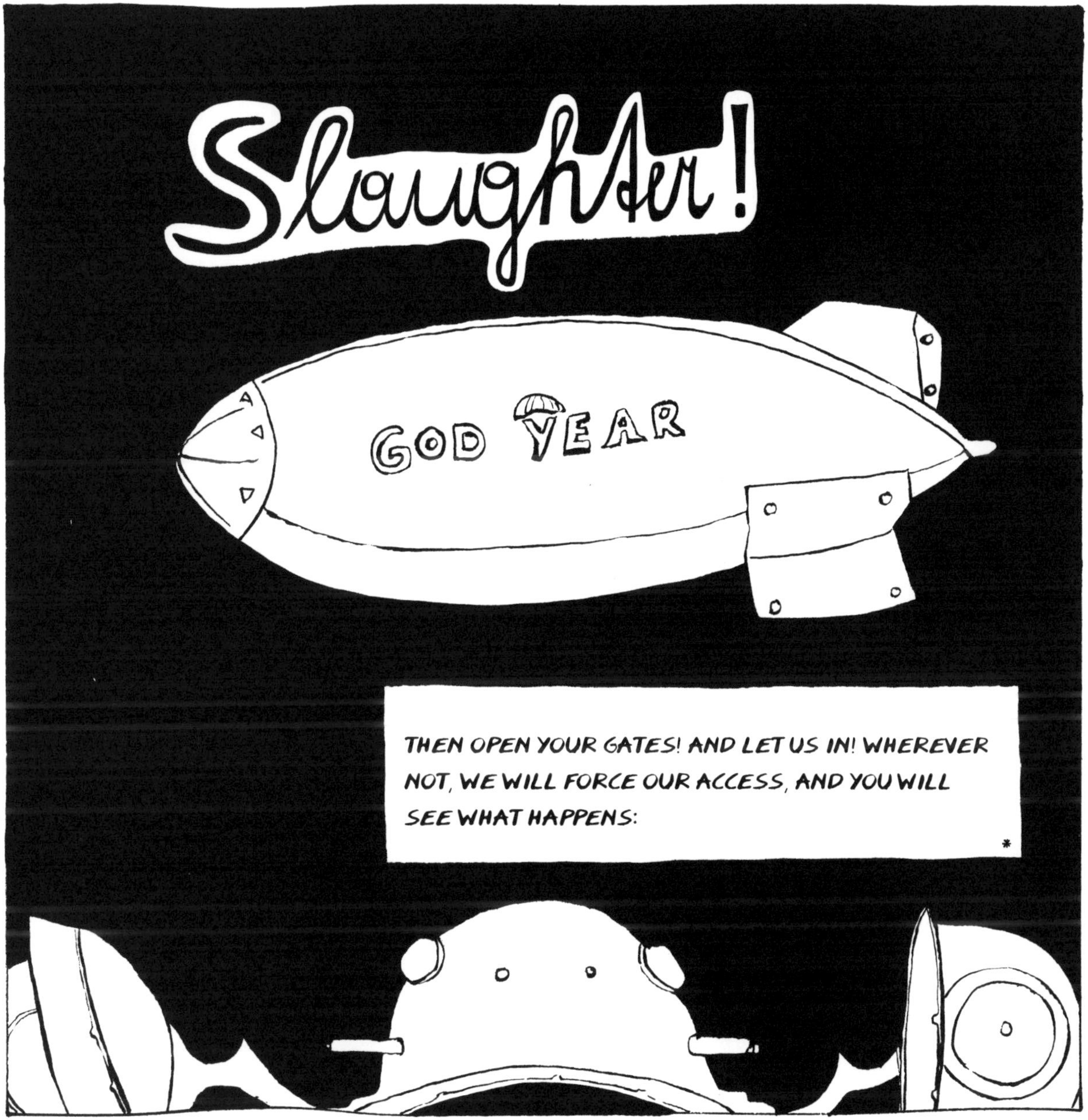
Slaughter!
GOD YEAR
THEN OPEN YOUR GATES! AND LET US IN! WHEREVER NOT, WE WILL FORCE OUR ACCESS, AND YOU WILL SEE WHAT HAPPENS:
*

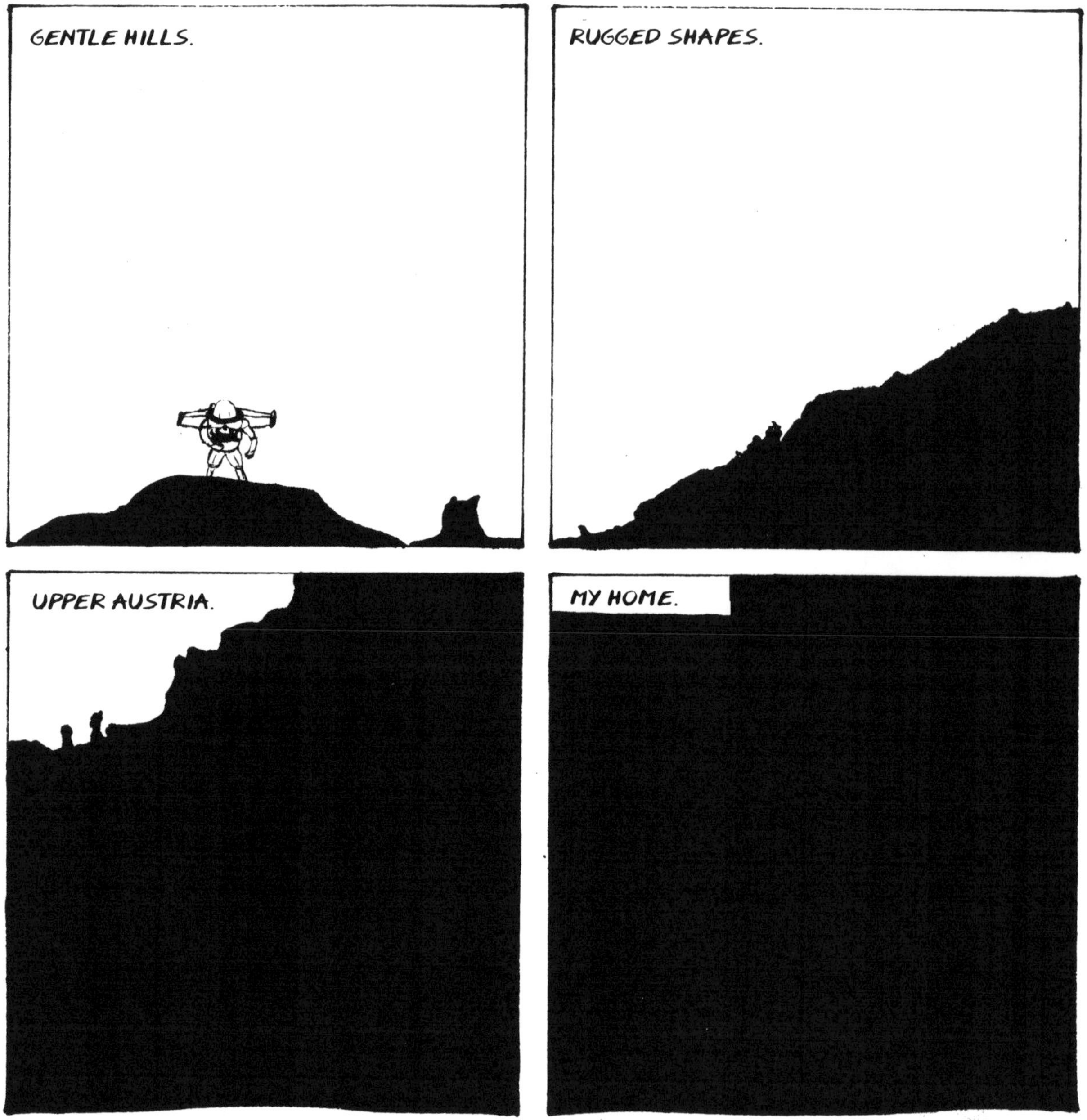
GENTLE HILLS.
RUGGED SHAPES.
UPPER AUSTRIA.
MY HOME.

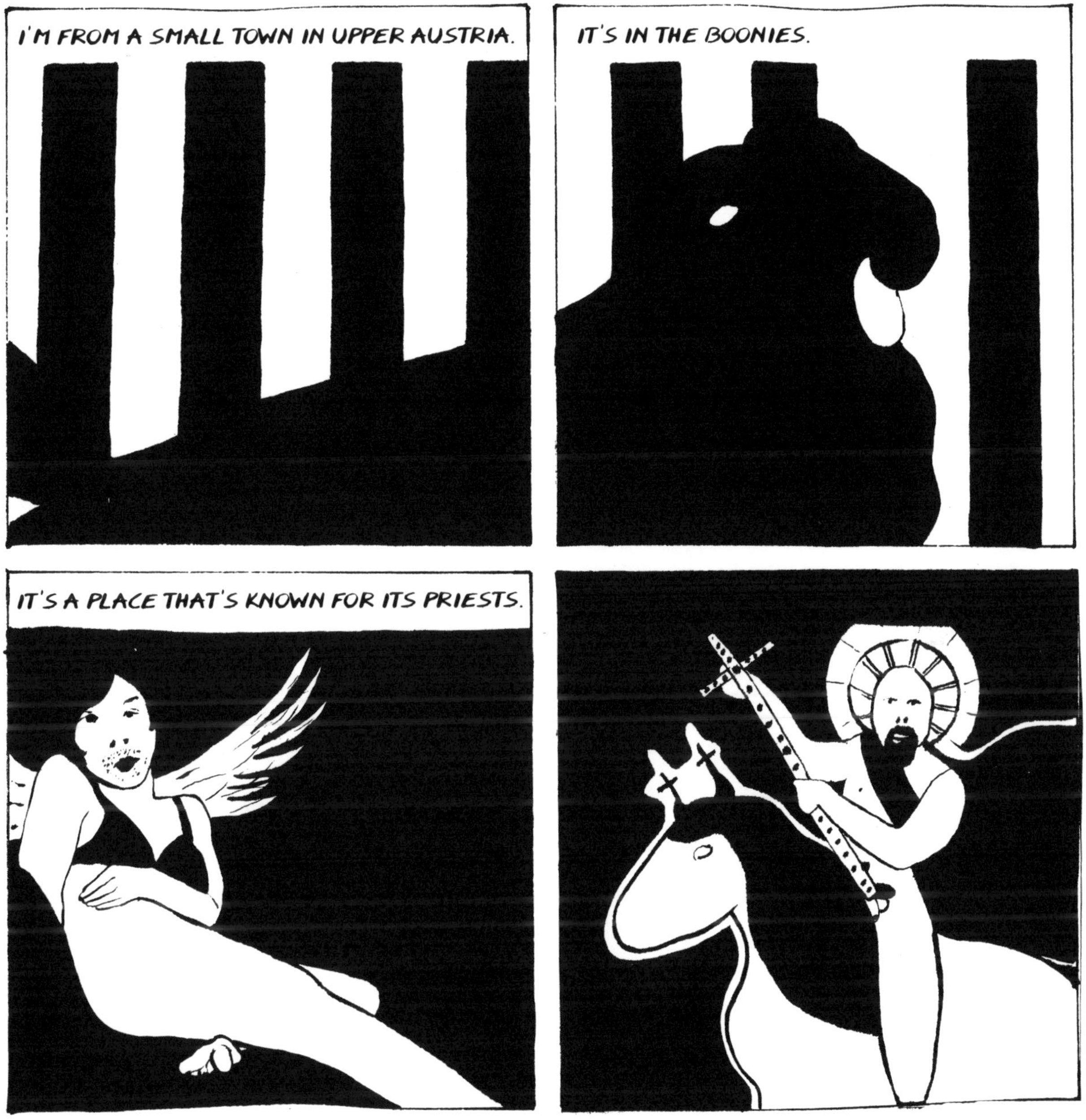
I'M FROM A SMALL TOWN IN UPPER AUSTRIA.
IT'S IN THE BOONIES.
IT'S A PLACE THAT'S KNOWN FOR ITS PRIESTS.

SOMETIMES, OUR PASTOR CLAIMED THAT KIDS WERE SHITTING IN THE PARISH FOREST.

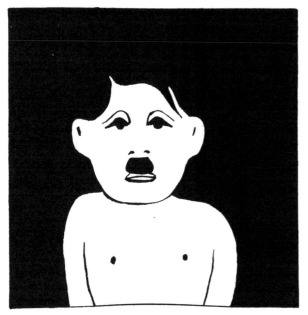

I WONDER WHY THAT'S SUCH A BIG DEAL.

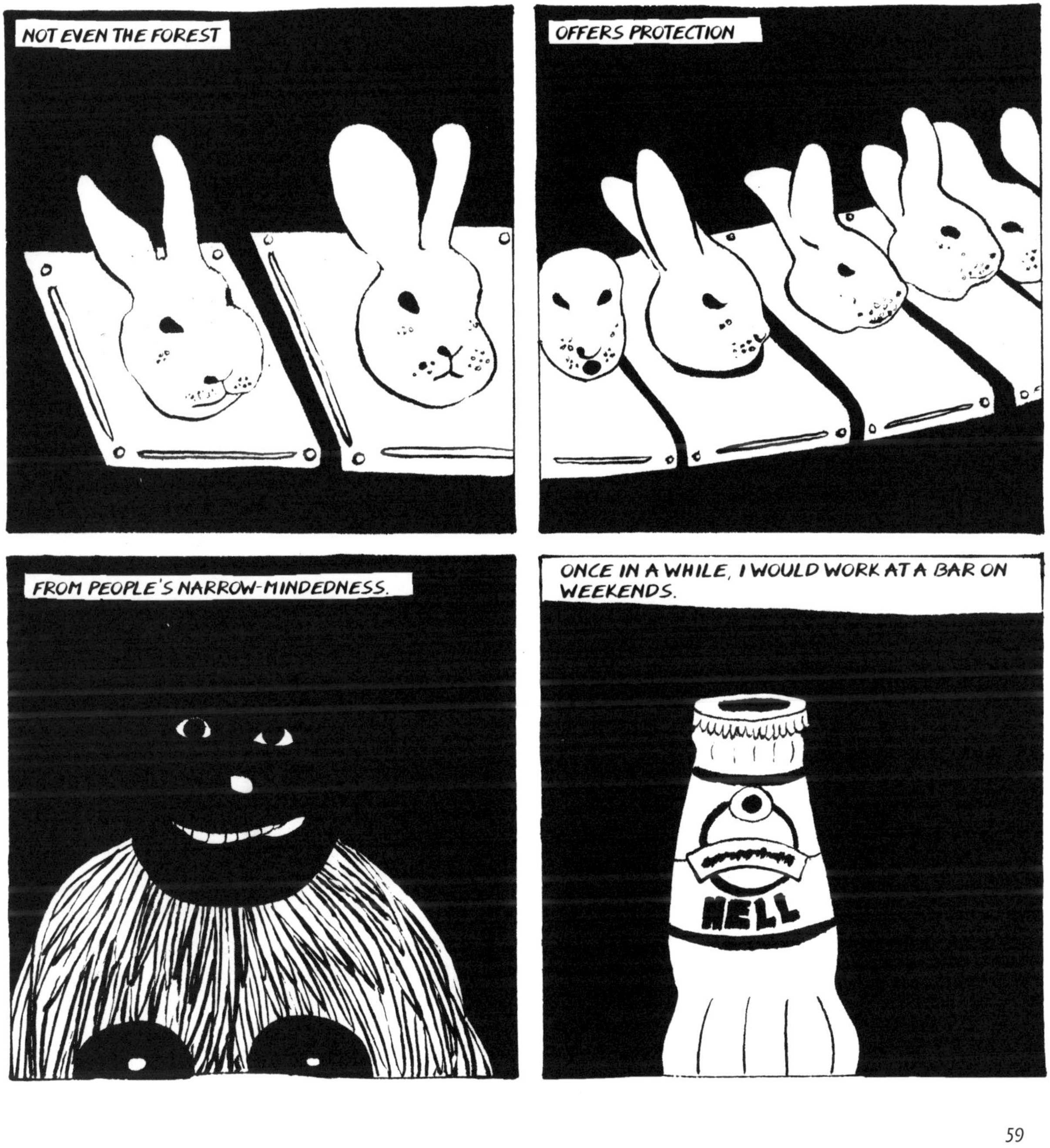
NOT EVEN THE FOREST
OFFERS PROTECTION
FROM PEOPLE'S NARROW-MINDEDNESS.
ONCE IN A WHILE, I WOULD WORK AT A BAR ON WEEKENDS.
HELL

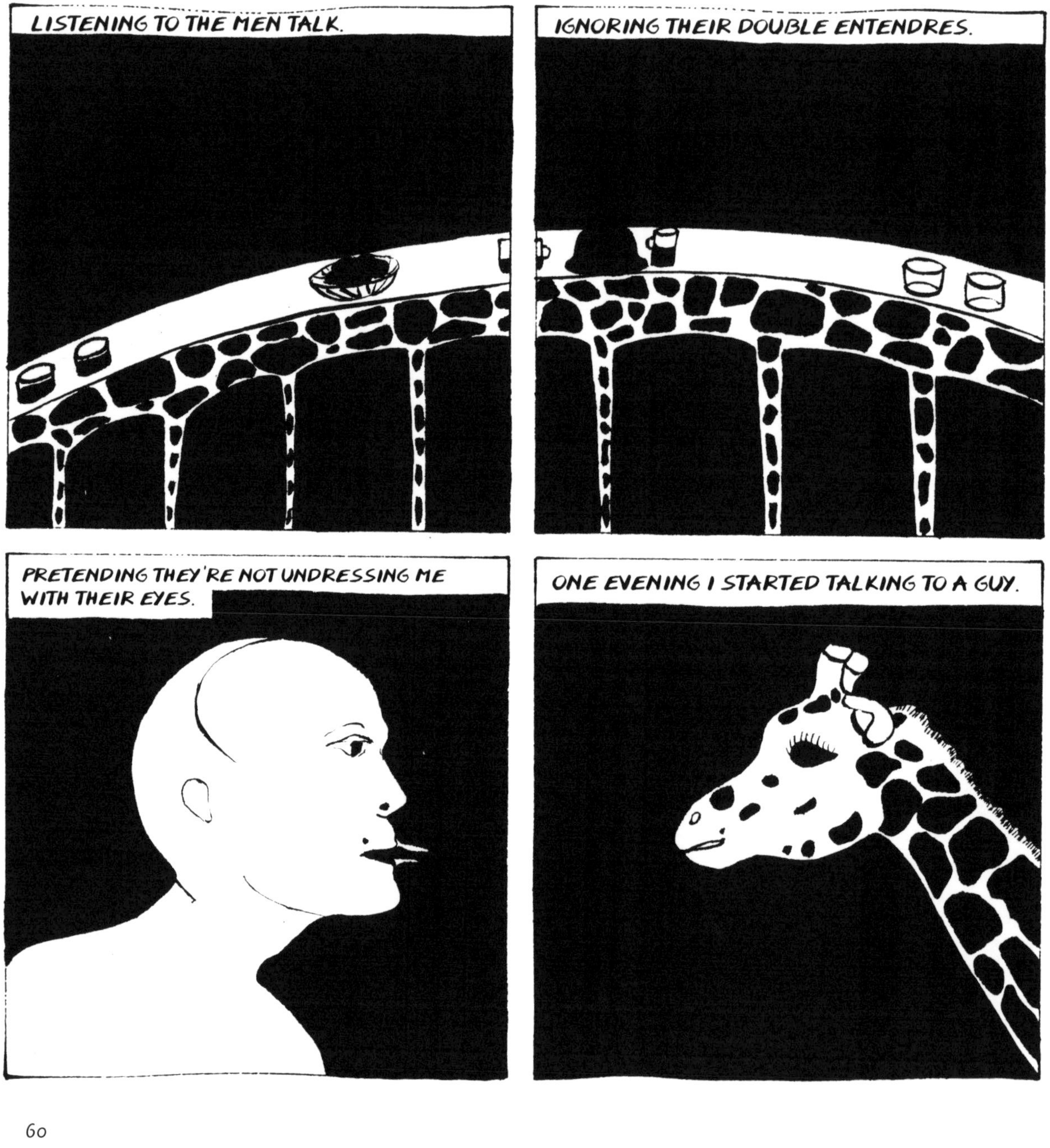
LISTENING TO THE MEN TALK.
IGNORING THEIR DOUBLE ENTENDRES.
PRETENDING THEY'RE NOT UNDRESSING ME WITH THEIR EYES.
ONE EVENING I STARTED TALKING TO A GUY.

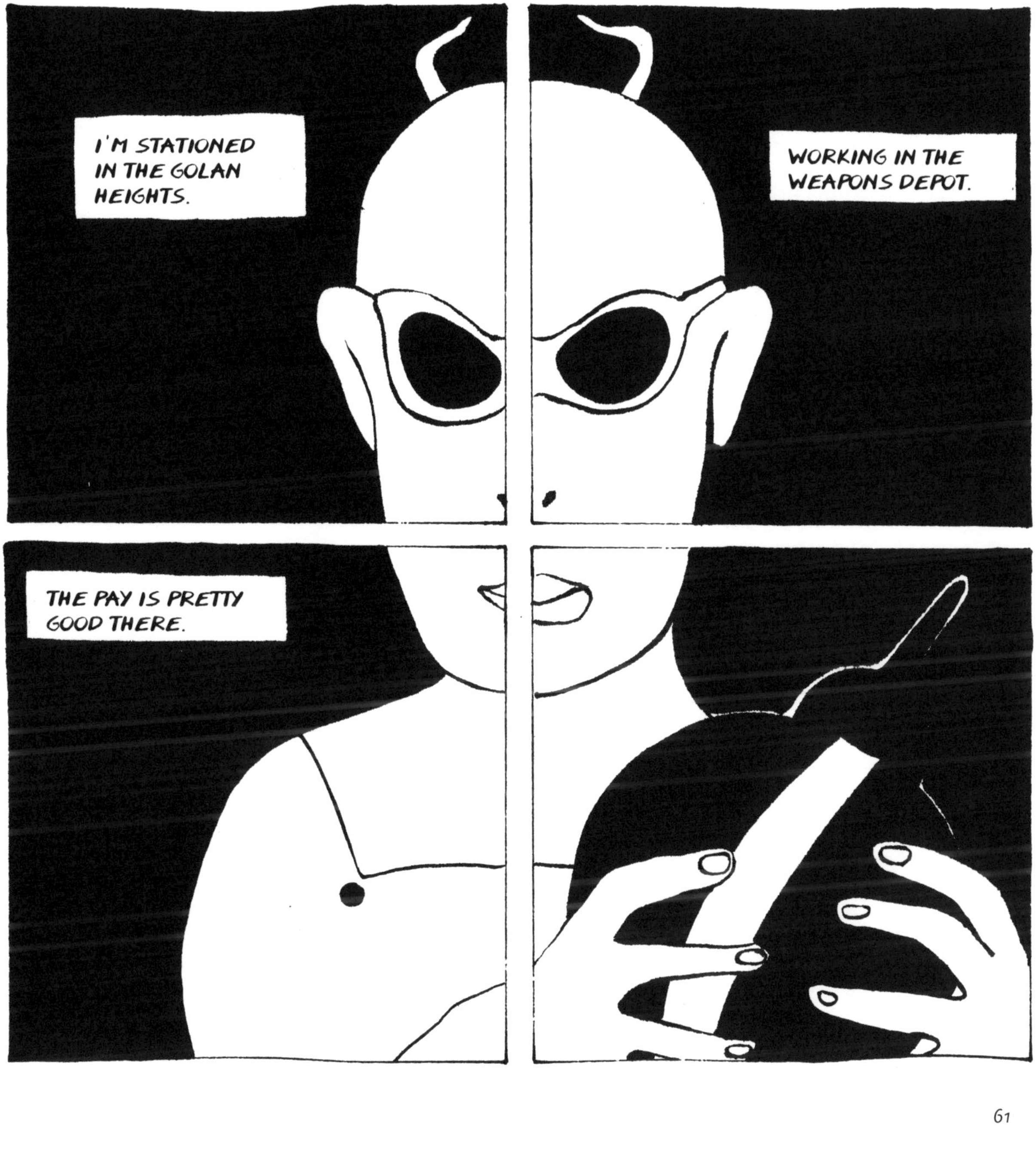
I'M STATIONED IN THE GOLAN HEIGHTS.
WORKING IN THE WEAPONS DEPOT.
THE PAY IS PRETTY GOOD THERE.

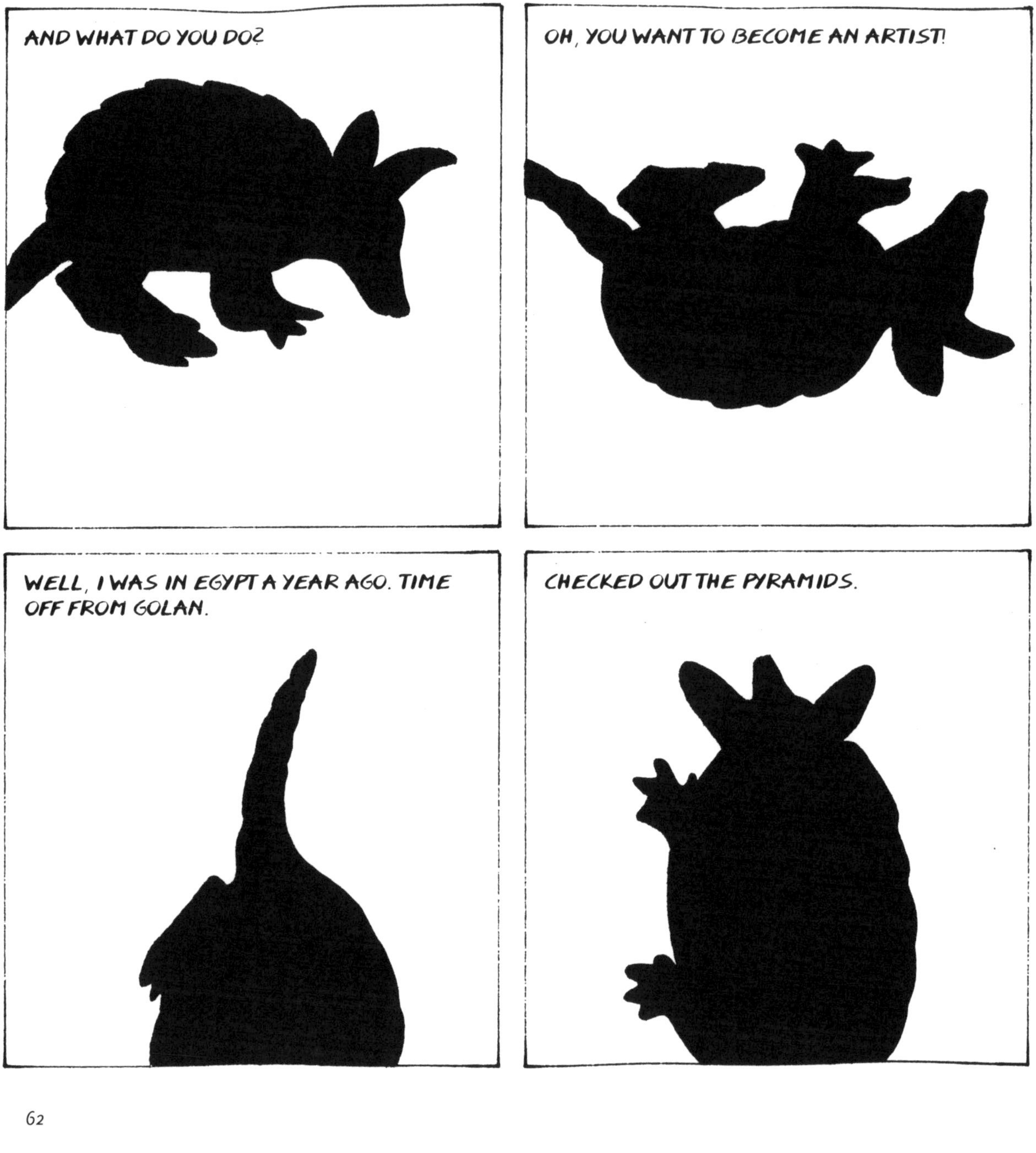
AND WHAT DO YOU DO?
OH, YOU WANT TO BECOME AN ARTIST!
WELL, I WAS IN EGYPT A YEAR AGO. TIME OFF FROM GOLAN.
CHECKED OUT THE PYRAMIDS.

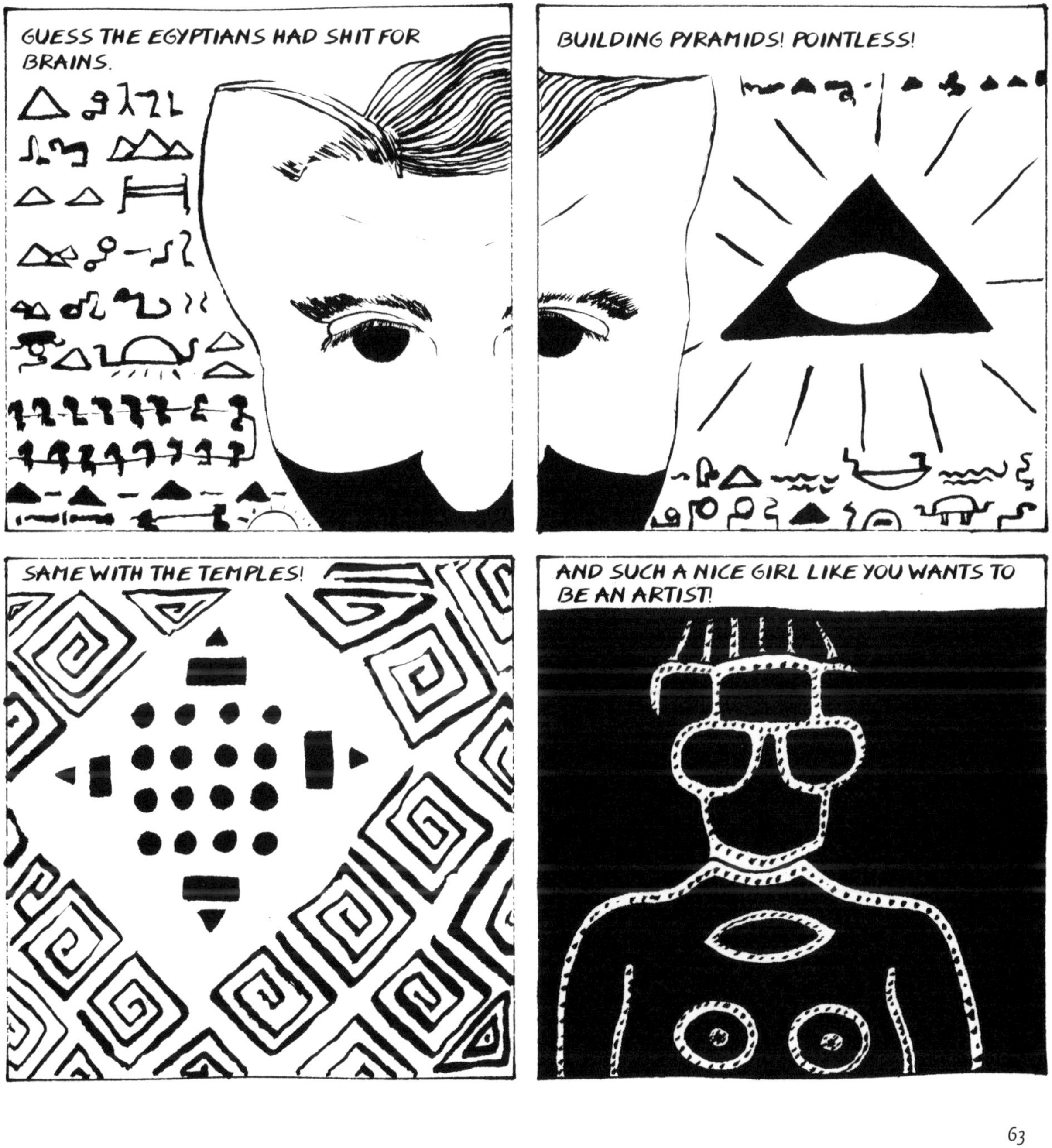
GUESS THE EGYPTIANS HAD SHIT FOR BRAINS.
BUILDING PYRAMIDS! POINTLESS!
SAME WITH THE TEMPLES!
AND SUCH A NICE GIRL LIKE YOU WANTS TO BE AN ARTIST!

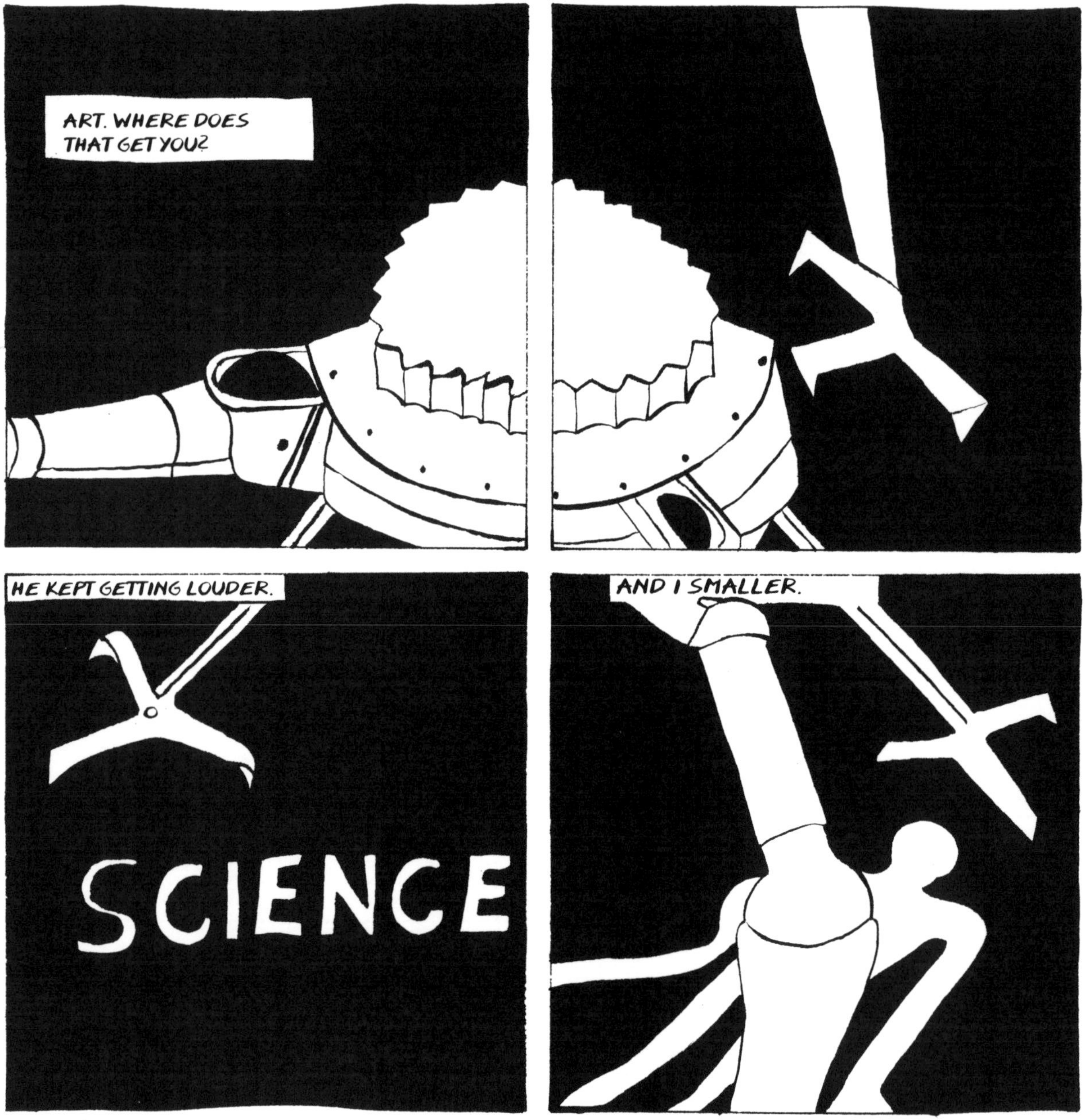
ART. WHERE DOES THAT GET YOU?
HE KEPT GETTING LOUDER.
SCIENCE
AND I SMALLER.

- FICTION

AT 18 I MOVED TO SALZBURG.

TO STUDY ART.

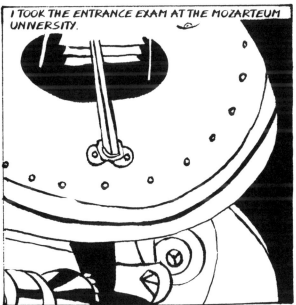

I TOOK THE ENTRANCE EXAM AT THE MOZARTEUM UNIVERSITY.

I PASSED AND ENROLLED IN ART EDUCATION.

MY PARENTS WERE HAPPY.

AT LEAST TEACHING IS A RESPECTABLE JOB.

SALZBURG SITS IN A VALLEY.

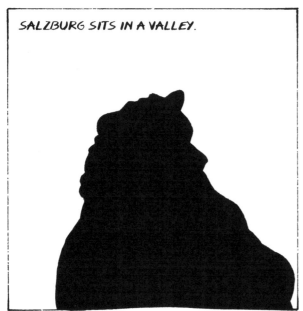

WHERE TWO CLIMATE ZONES COLLIDE.

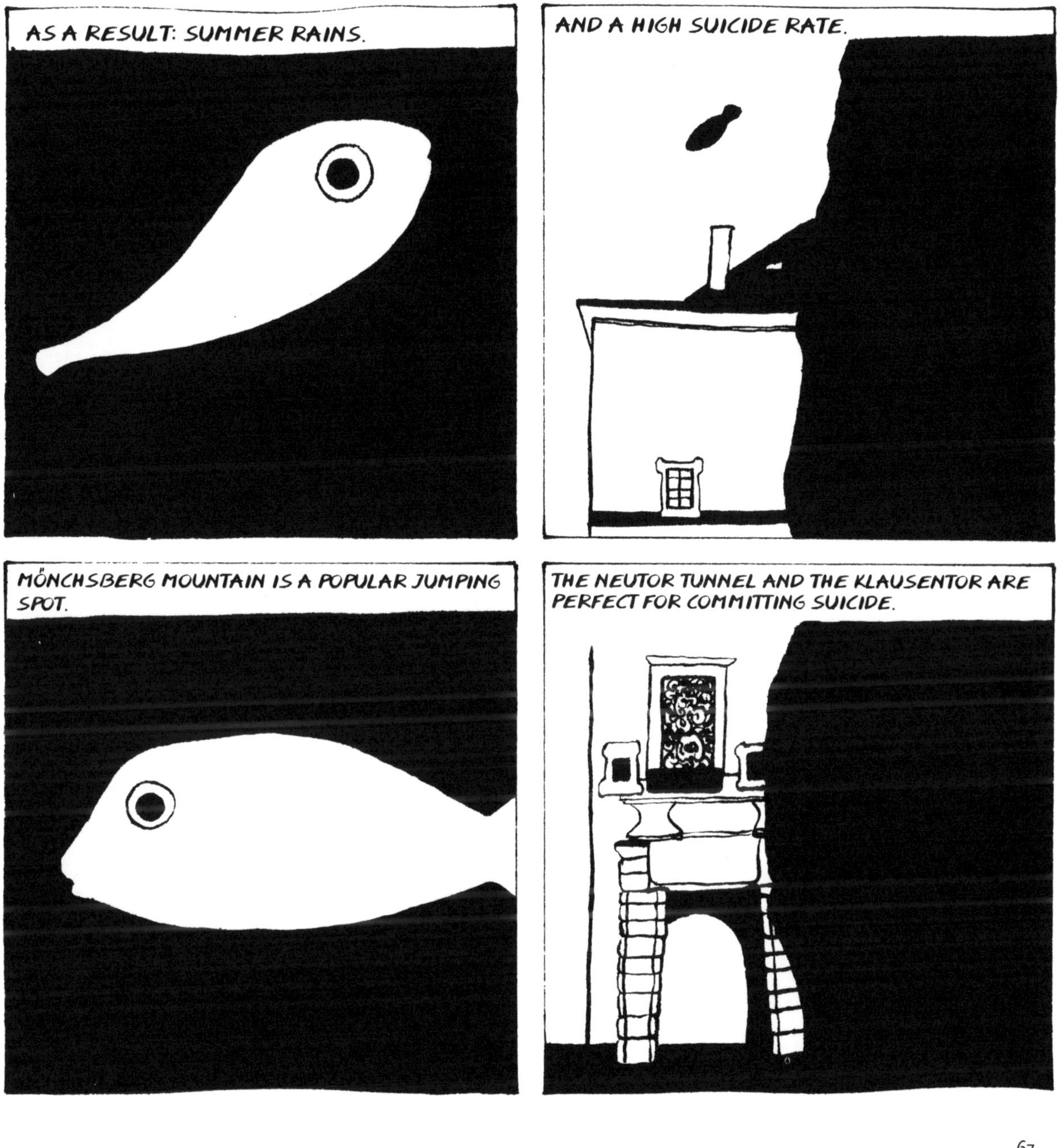
AS A RESULT: SUMMER RAINS.
AND A HIGH SUICIDE RATE.
MÖNCHSBERG MOUNTAIN IS A POPULAR JUMPING SPOT.
THE NEUTOR TUNNEL AND THE KLAUSENTOR ARE PERFECT FOR COMMITTING SUICIDE.

MY ART CLASSES WERE HELD ON THE CHRISTIAN-DOPPLER-STRASSE.

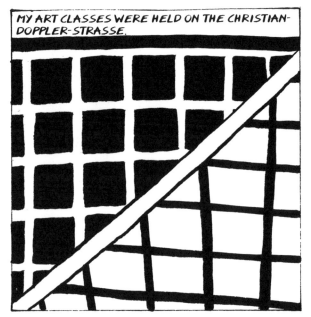

IN A FOUR-STORY STUDIO HOUSE.

Painting

Graphics

Sculpture

MY PROFESSOR SEEMED MORE LIKE AN ITALIAN THAN SOMEONE FROM SALZBURG.

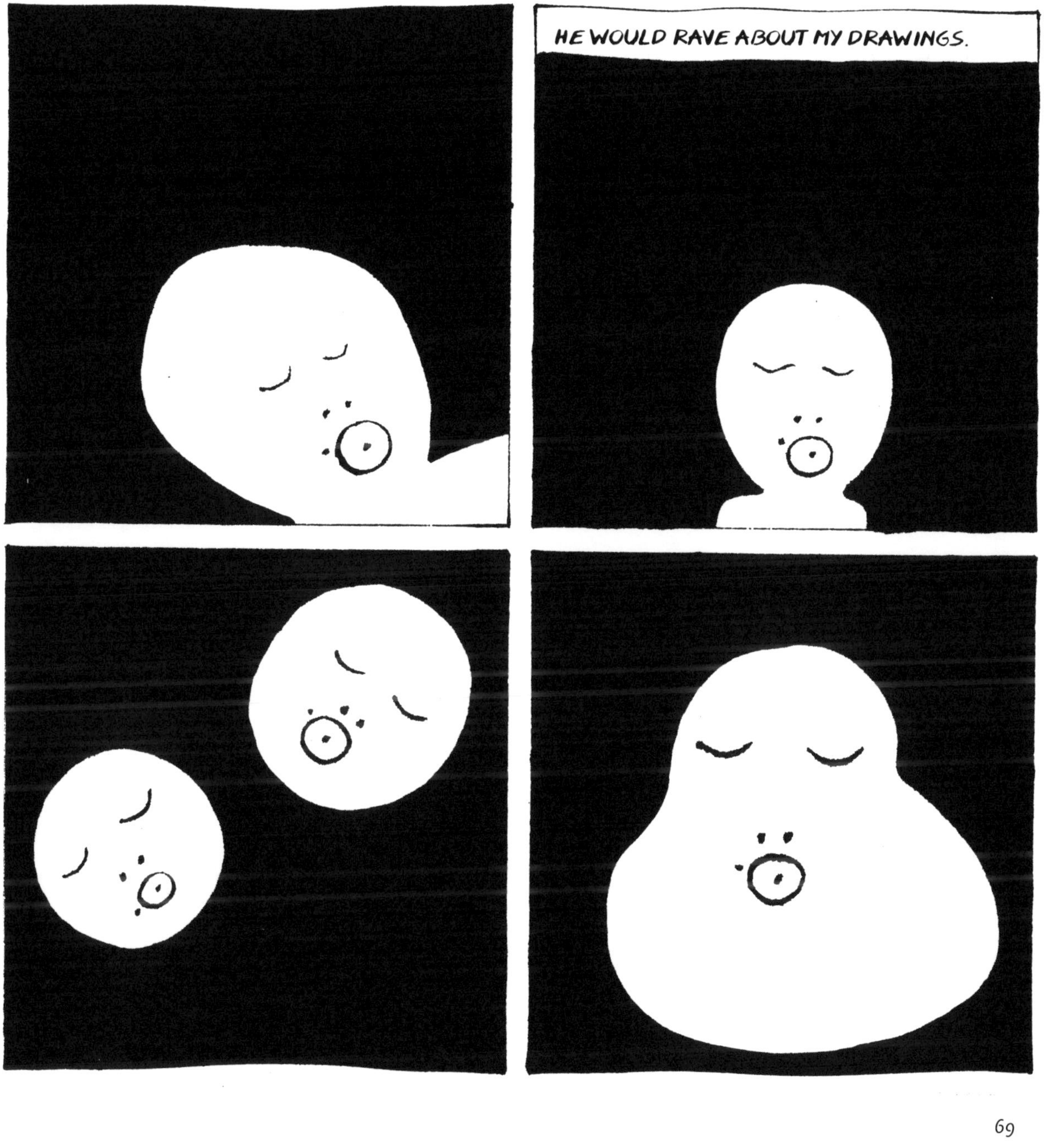
HE WOULD RAVE ABOUT MY DRAWINGS.

AND TALK ABOUT SICILY.

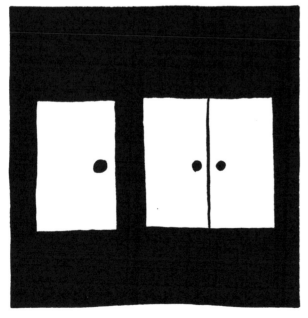

I LIVED IN A DORM, SHARING A PLACE WITH THREE OTHER GIRLS.

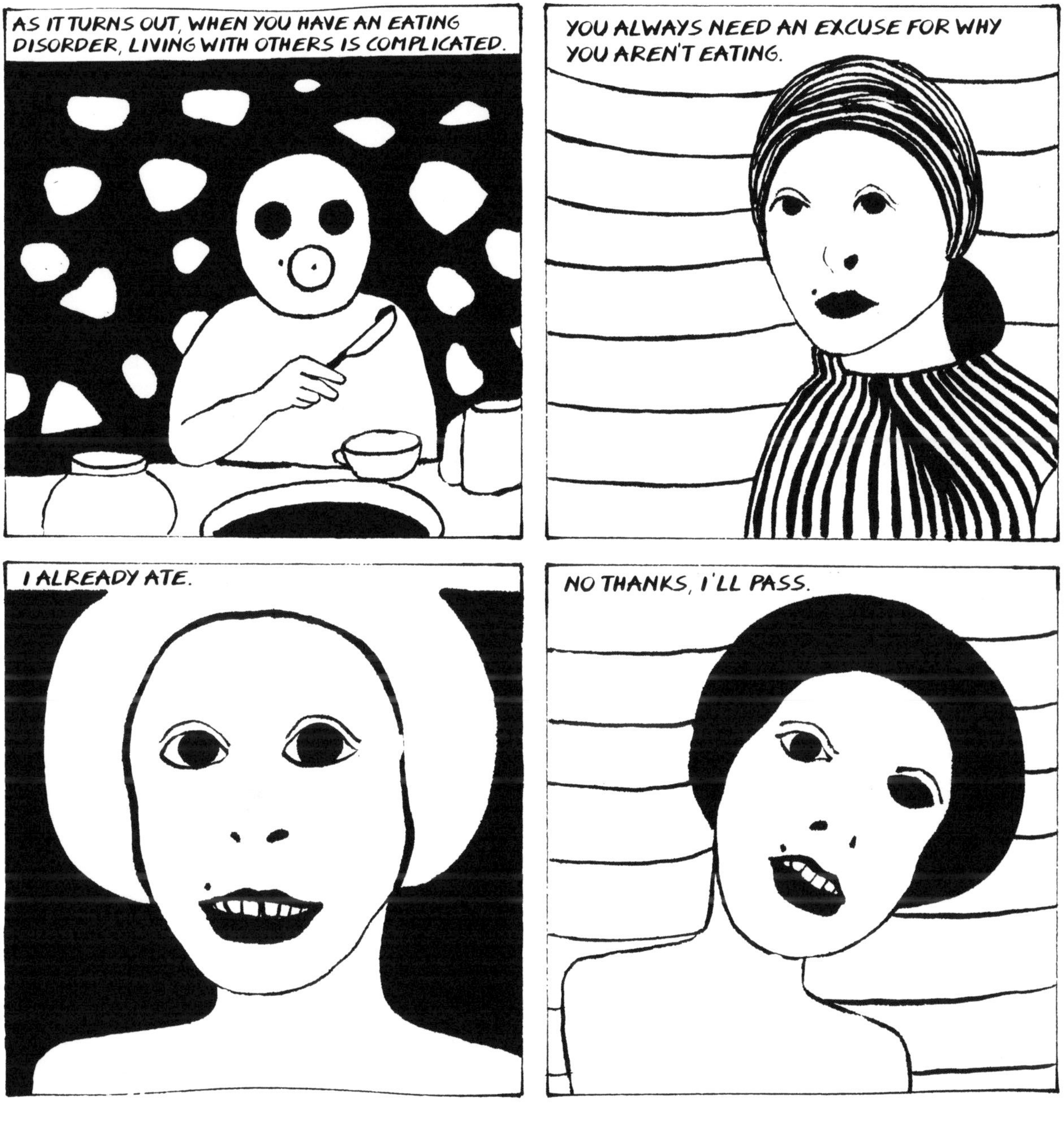
AS IT TURNS OUT, WHEN YOU HAVE AN EATING DISORDER, LIVING WITH OTHERS IS COMPLICATED.
YOU ALWAYS NEED AN EXCUSE FOR WHY YOU AREN'T EATING.
I ALREADY ATE.
NO THANKS, I'LL PASS.

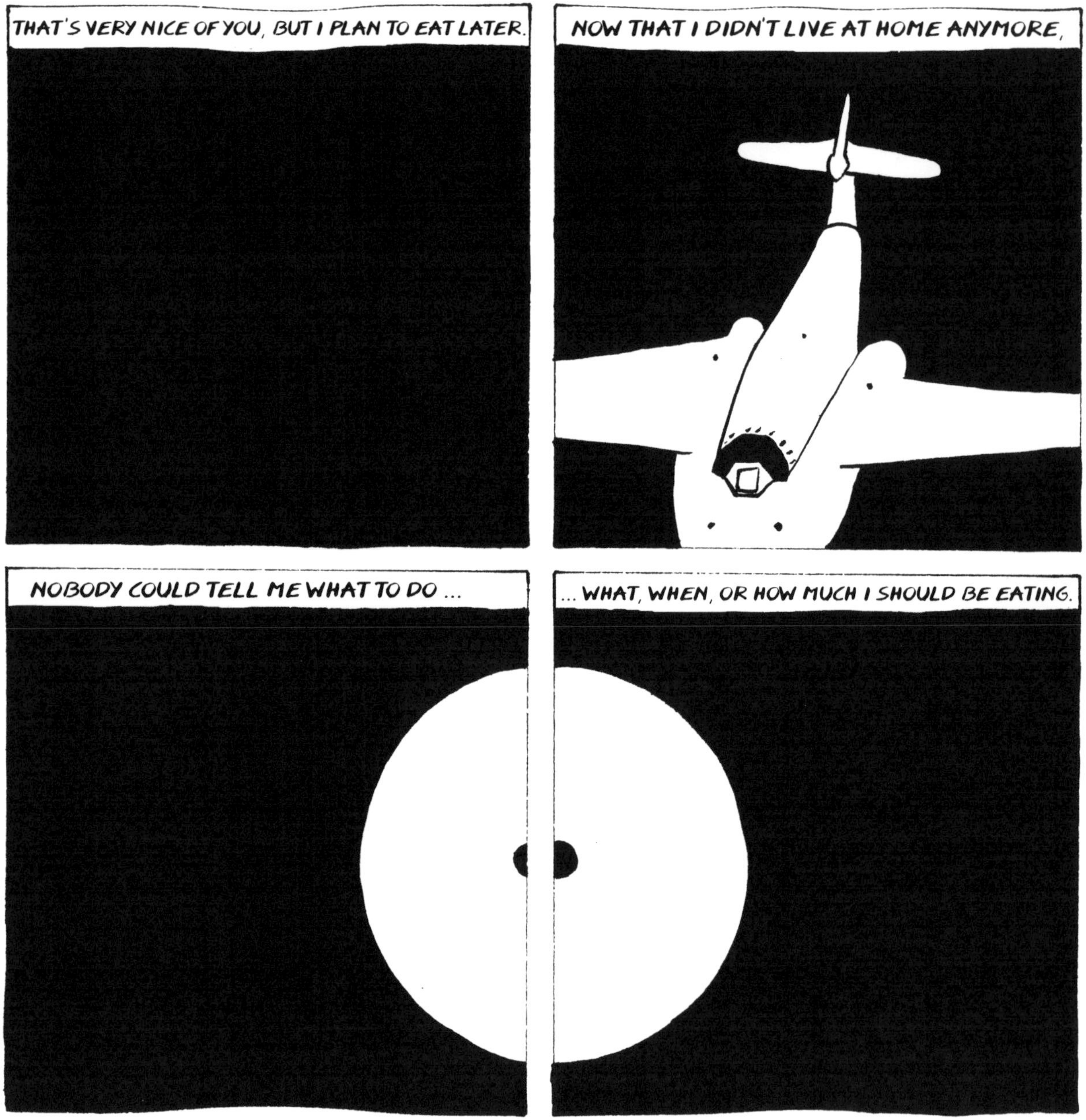
THAT'S VERY NICE OF YOU, BUT I PLAN TO EAT LATER.
NOW THAT I DIDN'T LIVE AT HOME ANYMORE,
NOBODY COULD TELL ME WHAT TO DO ...
... WHAT, WHEN, OR HOW MUCH I SHOULD BE EATING.

I THOUGHT EVERYTHING WOULD GET EASIER.

I MANAGED TO KEEP MY EATING DISORDER A SECRET FOR THREE YEARS.

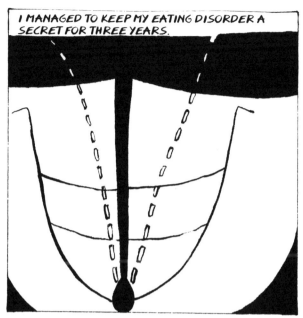

NOBODY NOTICED ANYTHING.

I WITHDREW MORE AND MORE INTO MYSELF.

BUT ON THE OUTSIDE, I WAS A RAY OF SUNSHINE.

SOON, I WAS VERY POPULAR AT THE UNIVERSITY.

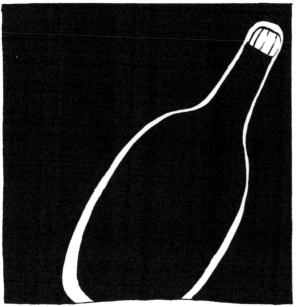

I HAD A REPUTATION AS A HIP ARTIST, ON THE RISE.

EXHIBITION ON NOW !

PRINTS AND DRAWINGS BY REGINA HOFER

ARTHOUSE
SALZBURG
OPEN DAILY

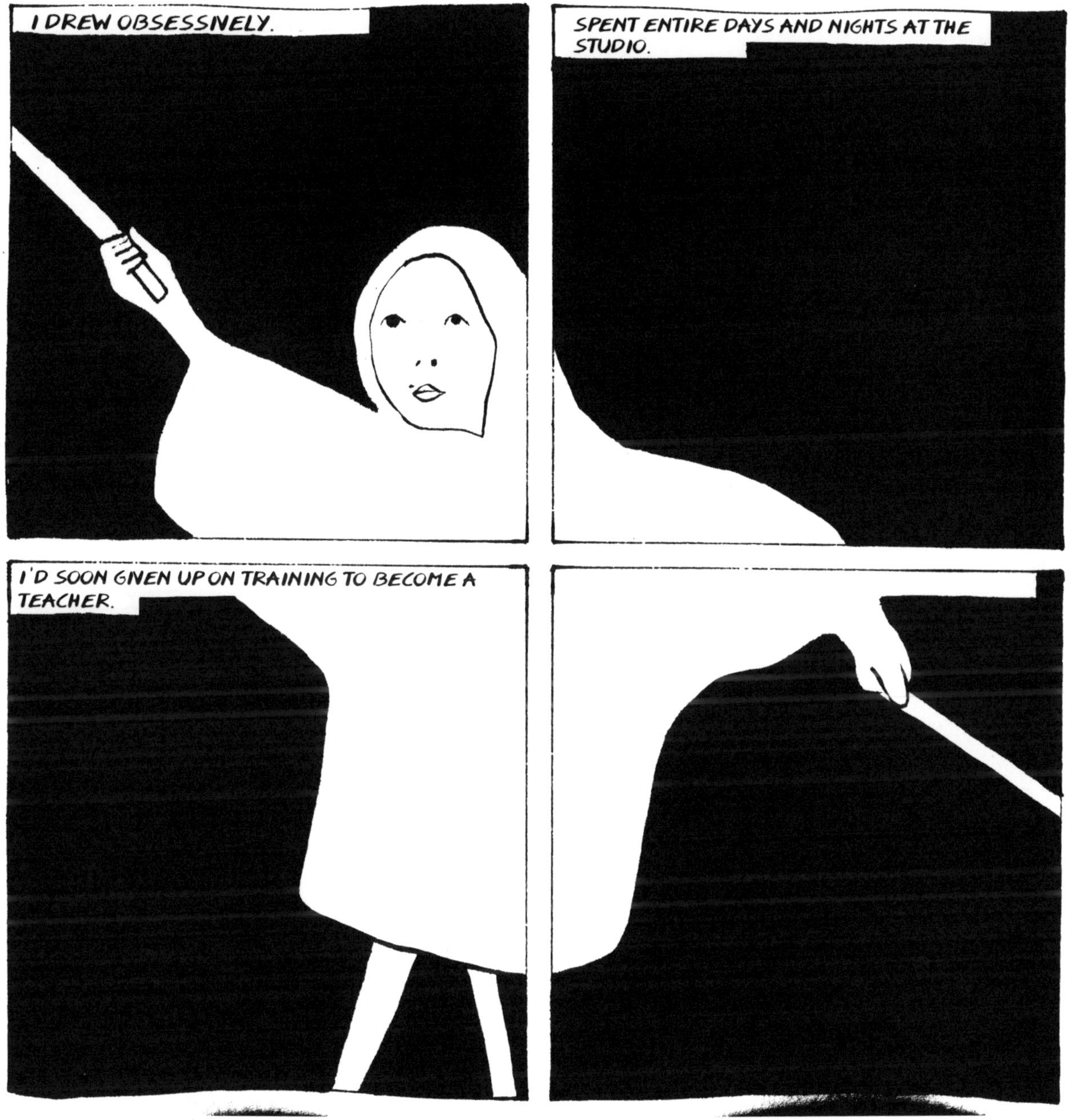
I DREW OBSESSIVELY.
SPENT ENTIRE DAYS AND NIGHTS AT THE STUDIO.
I'D SOON GIVEN UP ON TRAINING TO BECOME A TEACHER.

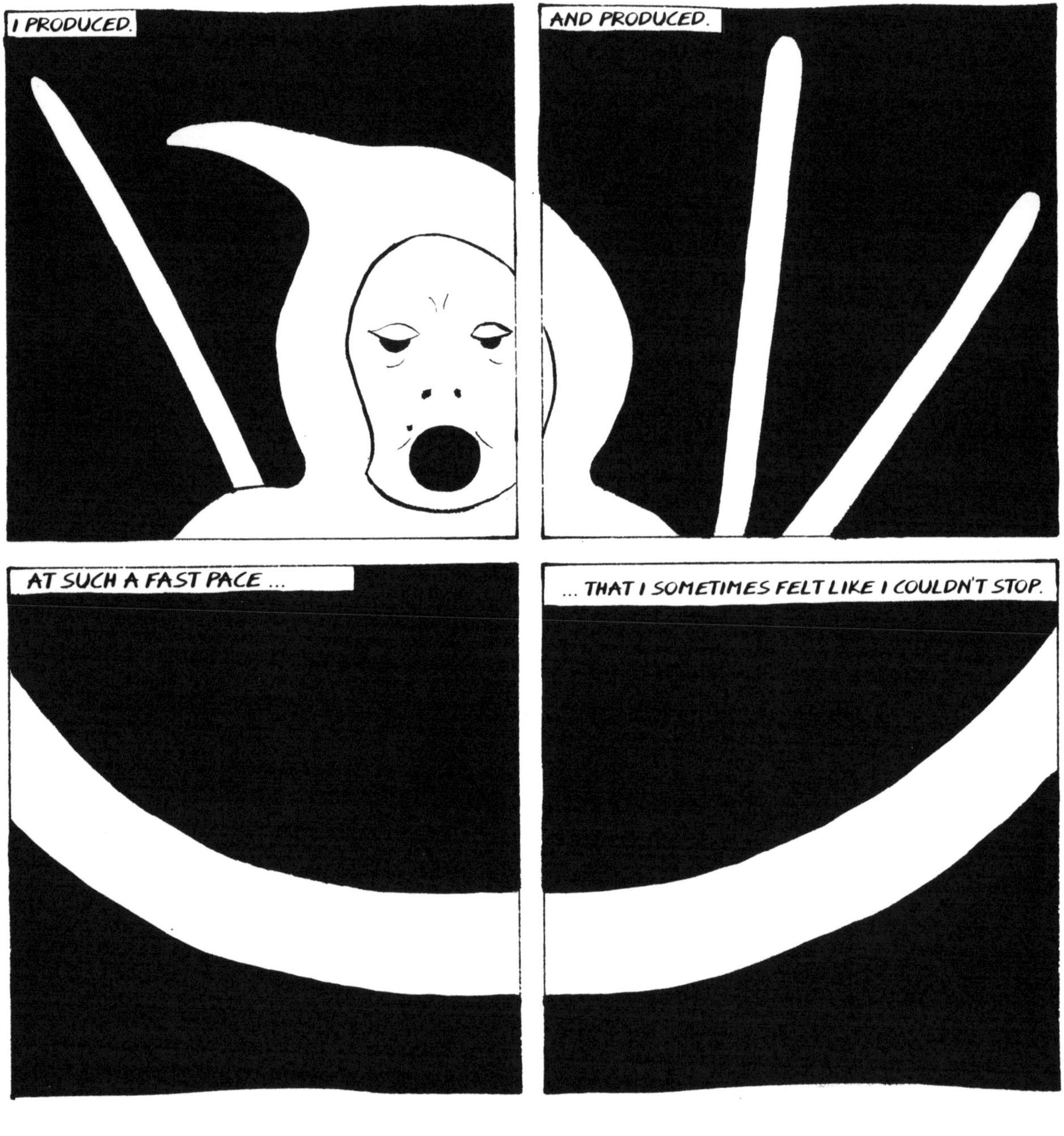
I PRODUCED.
AND PRODUCED.
AT SUCH A FAST PACE ...
... THAT I SOMETIMES FELT LIKE I COULDN'T STOP.

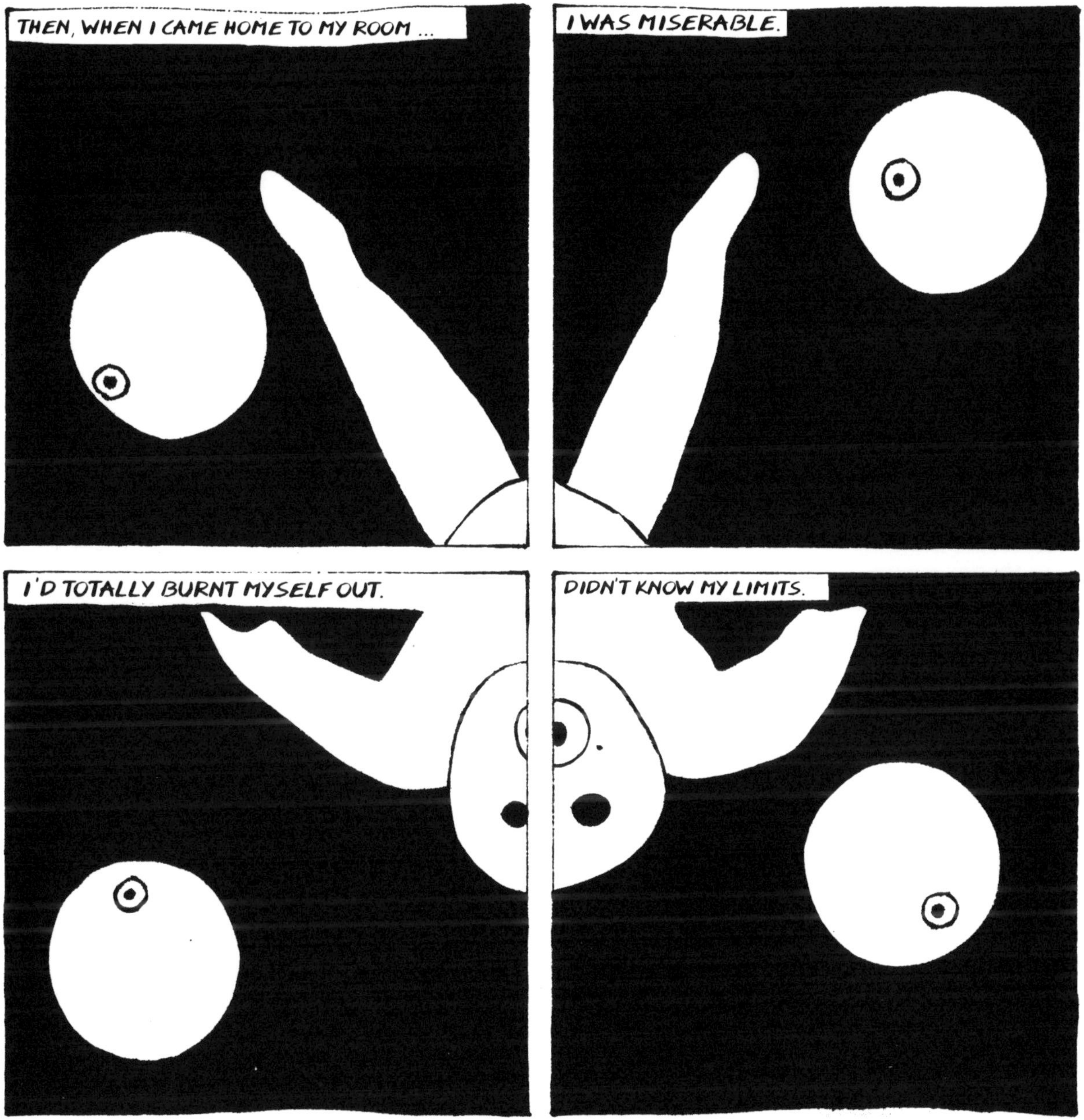
THEN, WHEN I CAME HOME TO MY ROOM ...
I WAS MISERABLE.
I'D TOTALLY BURNT MYSELF OUT.
DIDN'T KNOW MY LIMITS.

WORKING TO THE POINT OF PASSING OUT.

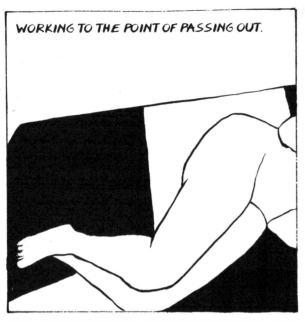

PROVING TO MY DAD THAT I WAS GOING TO MAKE IT.

I WAS TIRED OF STARVING MYSELF ...

... ONLY TO START BINGEING AGAIN.

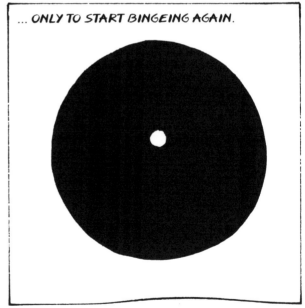

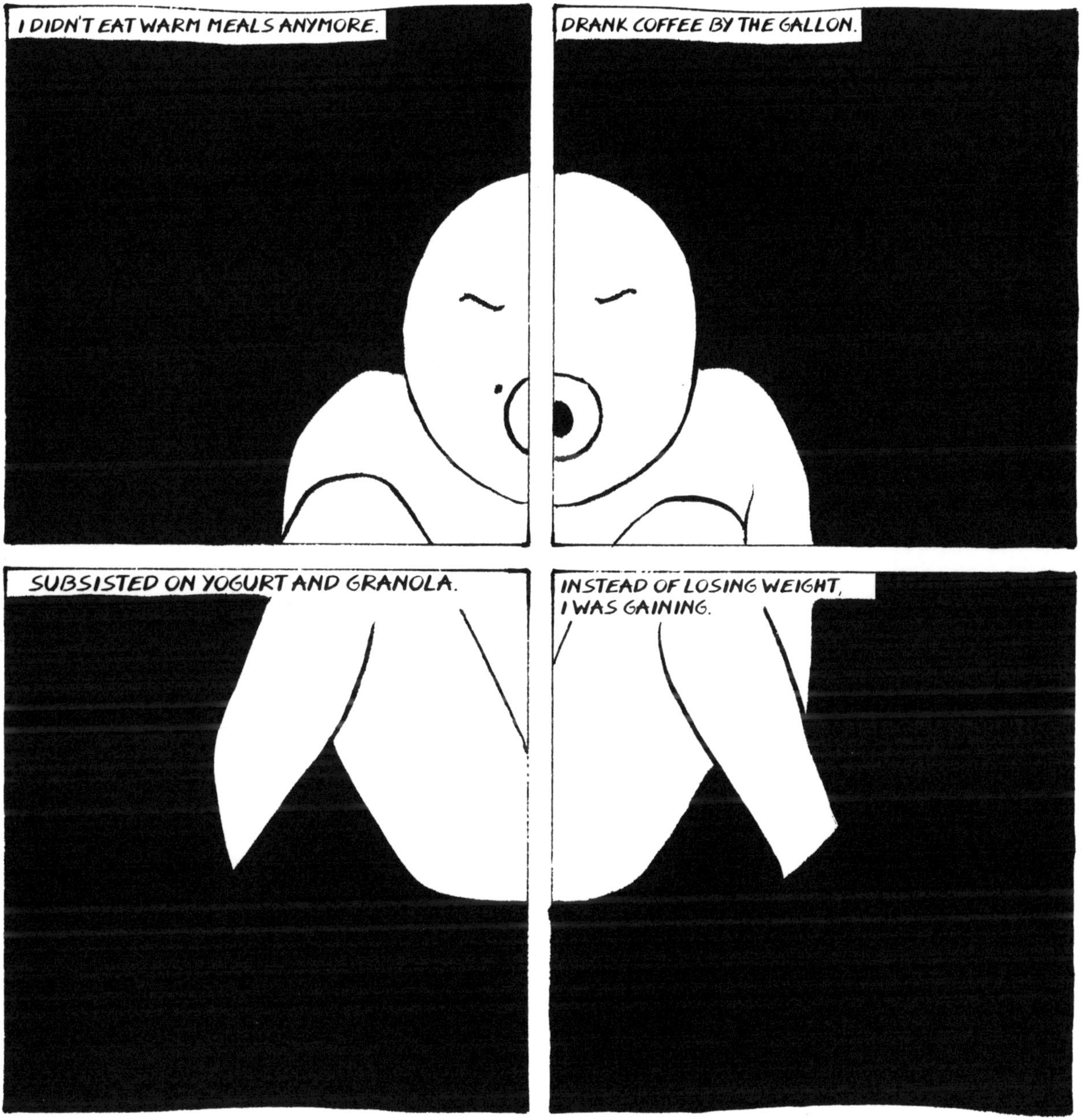
I DIDN'T EAT WARM MEALS ANYMORE.
DRANK COFFEE BY THE GALLON.
SUBSISTED ON YOGURT AND GRANOLA.
INSTEAD OF LOSING WEIGHT, I WAS GAINING.

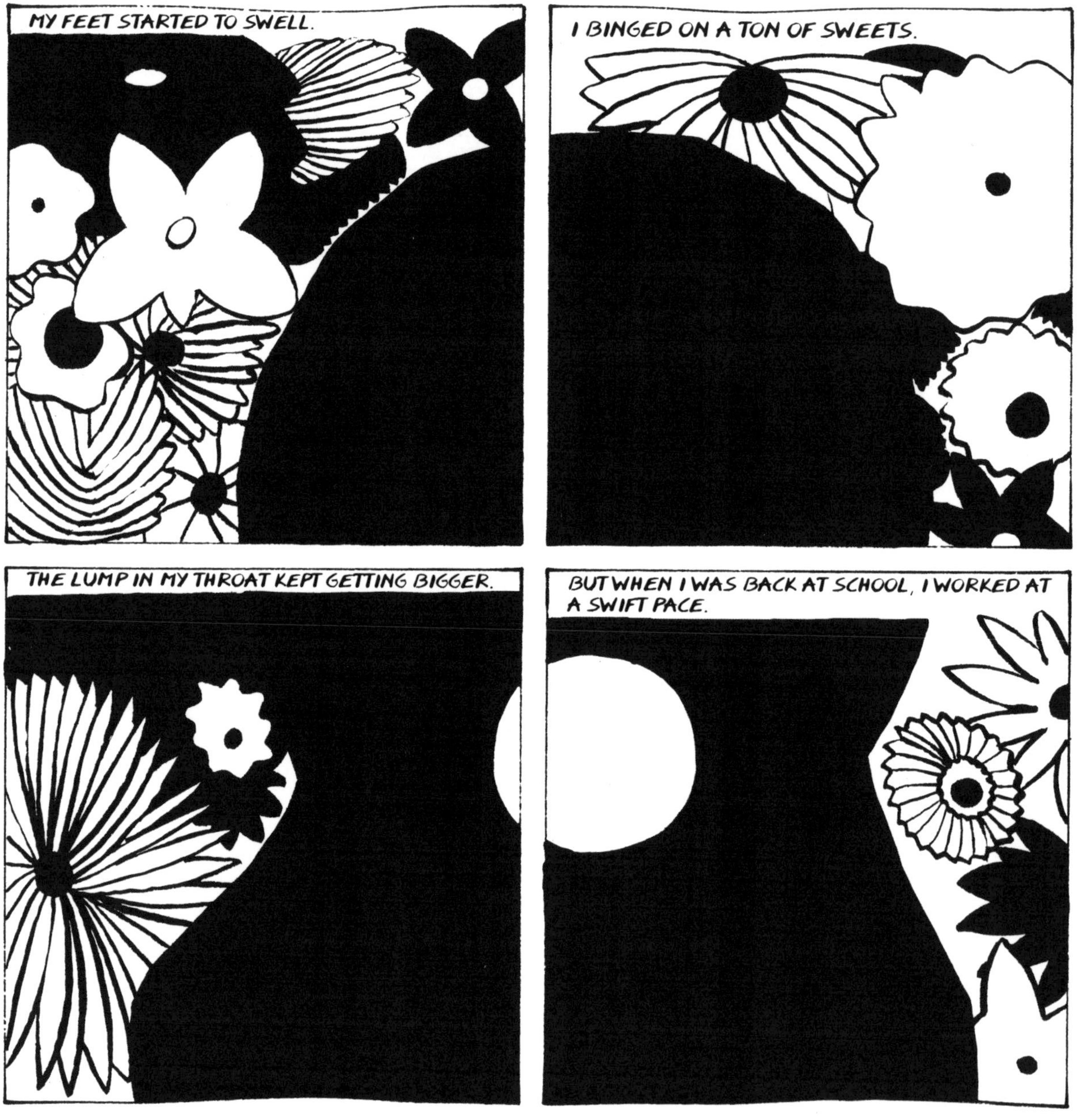
MY FEET STARTED TO SWELL.
I BINGED ON A TON OF SWEETS.
THE LUMP IN MY THROAT KEPT GETTING BIGGER.
BUT WHEN I WAS BACK AT SCHOOL, I WORKED AT A SWIFT PACE.

I LIVED IN SALZBURG FOR THREE YEARS.

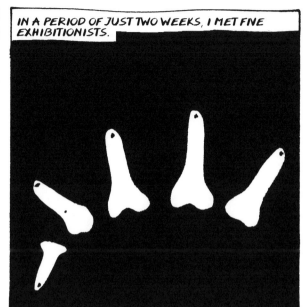

IN A PERIOD OF JUST TWO WEEKS, I MET FIVE EXHIBITIONISTS.

AT THE UNIVERSITY.

ON THE BUS.

ALONG THE RIVER.
AT THE TIME, I WAS DRAWING HONEYDEW MELONS.
PARDON ME, YOUNG LADY! AREN'T YOU FROM UPPER AUSTRIA?
I CAN TELL BY THE WAY YOU WALK.

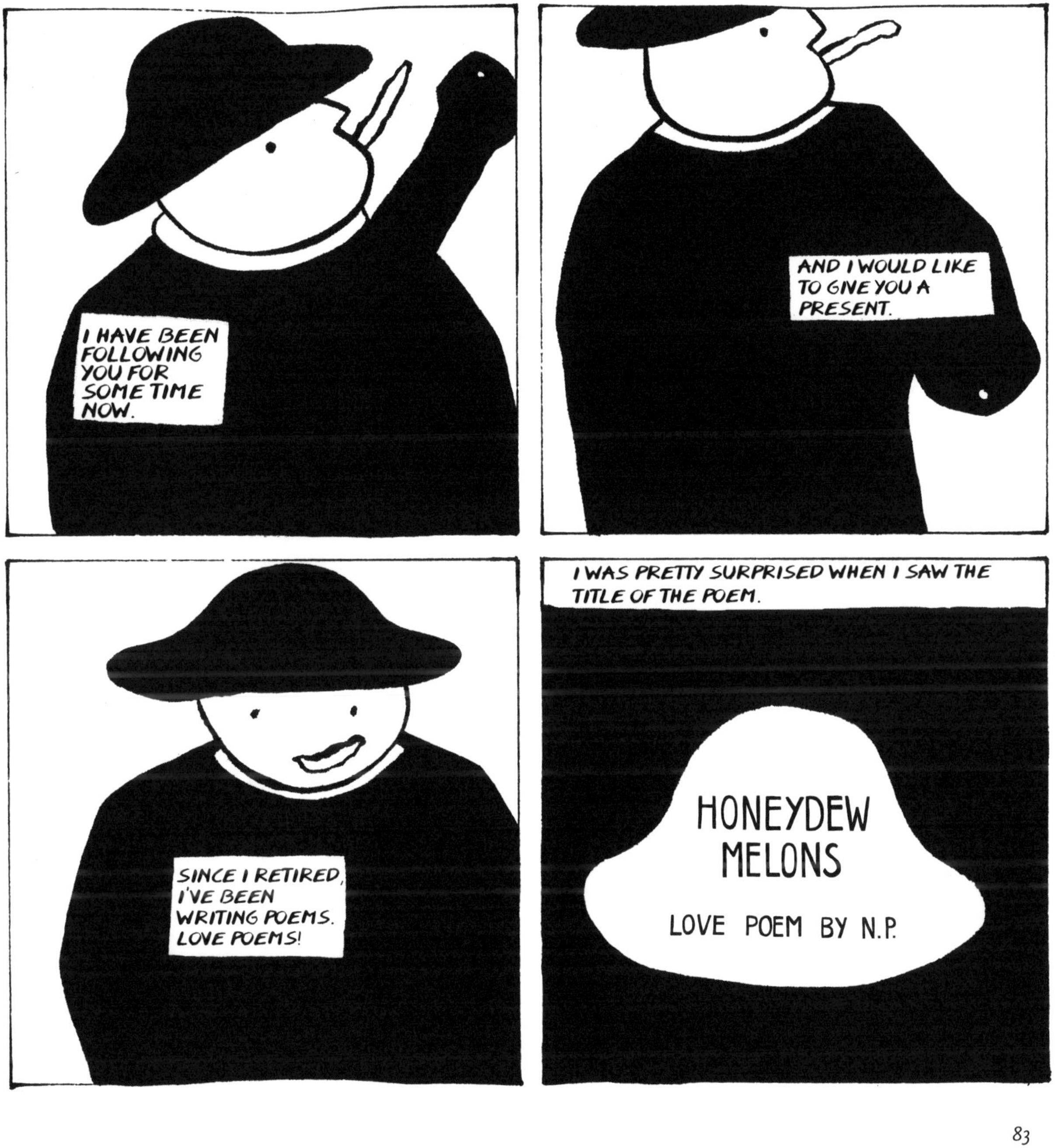
I HAVE BEEN FOLLOWING YOU FOR SOME TIME NOW.
AND I WOULD LIKE TO GIVE YOU A PRESENT.
SINCE I RETIRED, I'VE BEEN WRITING POEMS. LOVE POEMS!
I WAS PRETTY SURPRISED WHEN I SAW THE TITLE OF THE POEM.
HONEYDEW MELONS
LOVE POEM BY N.P.

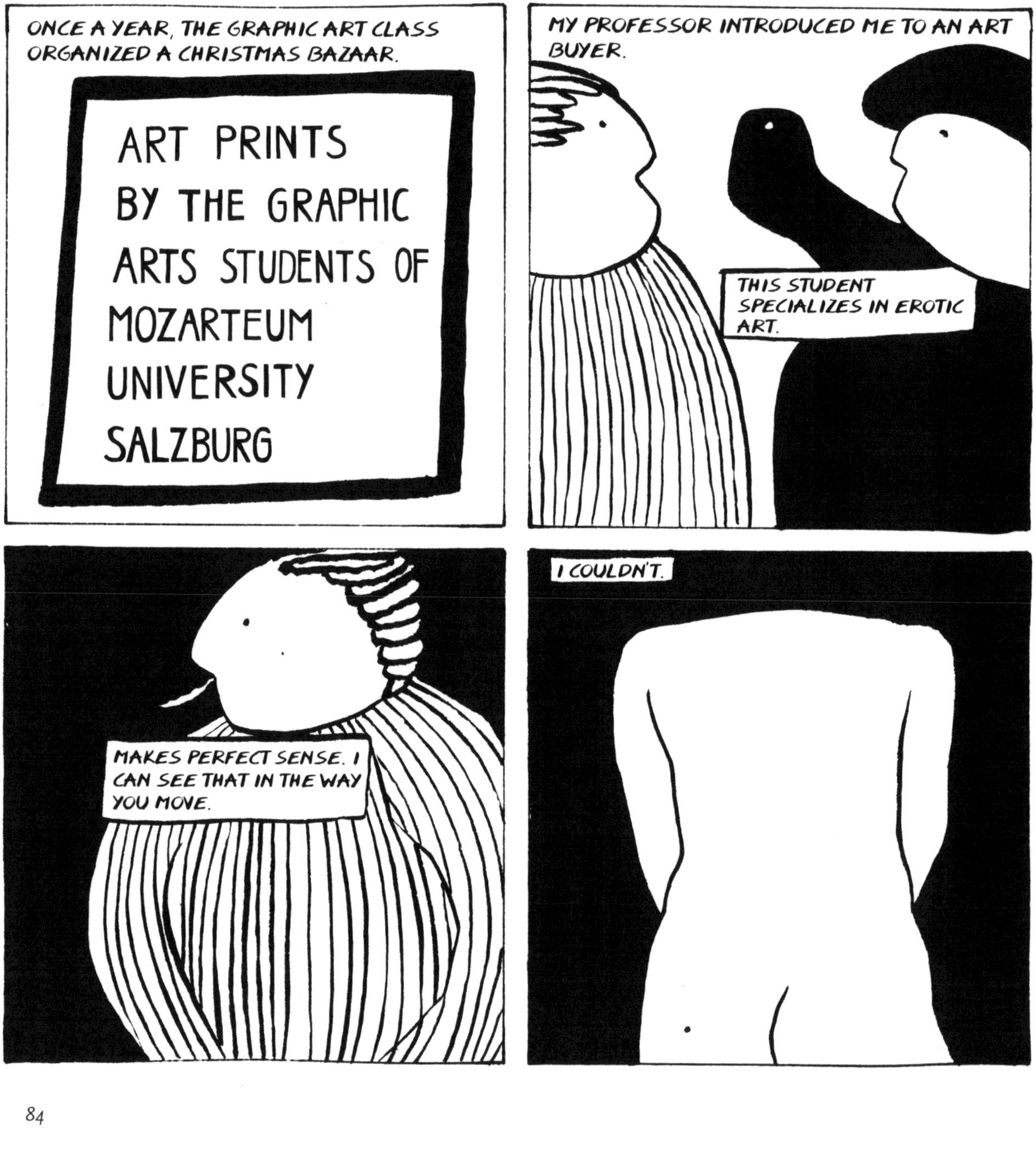
ONCE A YEAR, THE GRAPHIC ART CLASS ORGANIZED A CHRISTMAS BAZAAR.
ART PRINTS BY THE GRAPHIC ARTS STUDENTS OF MOZARTEUM UNIVERSITY SALZBURG
MY PROFESSOR INTRODUCED ME TO AN ART BUYER.
THIS STUDENT SPECIALIZES IN EROTIC ART.
MAKES PERFECT SENSE. I CAN SEE THAT IN THE WAY YOU MOVE.
I COULDN'T.

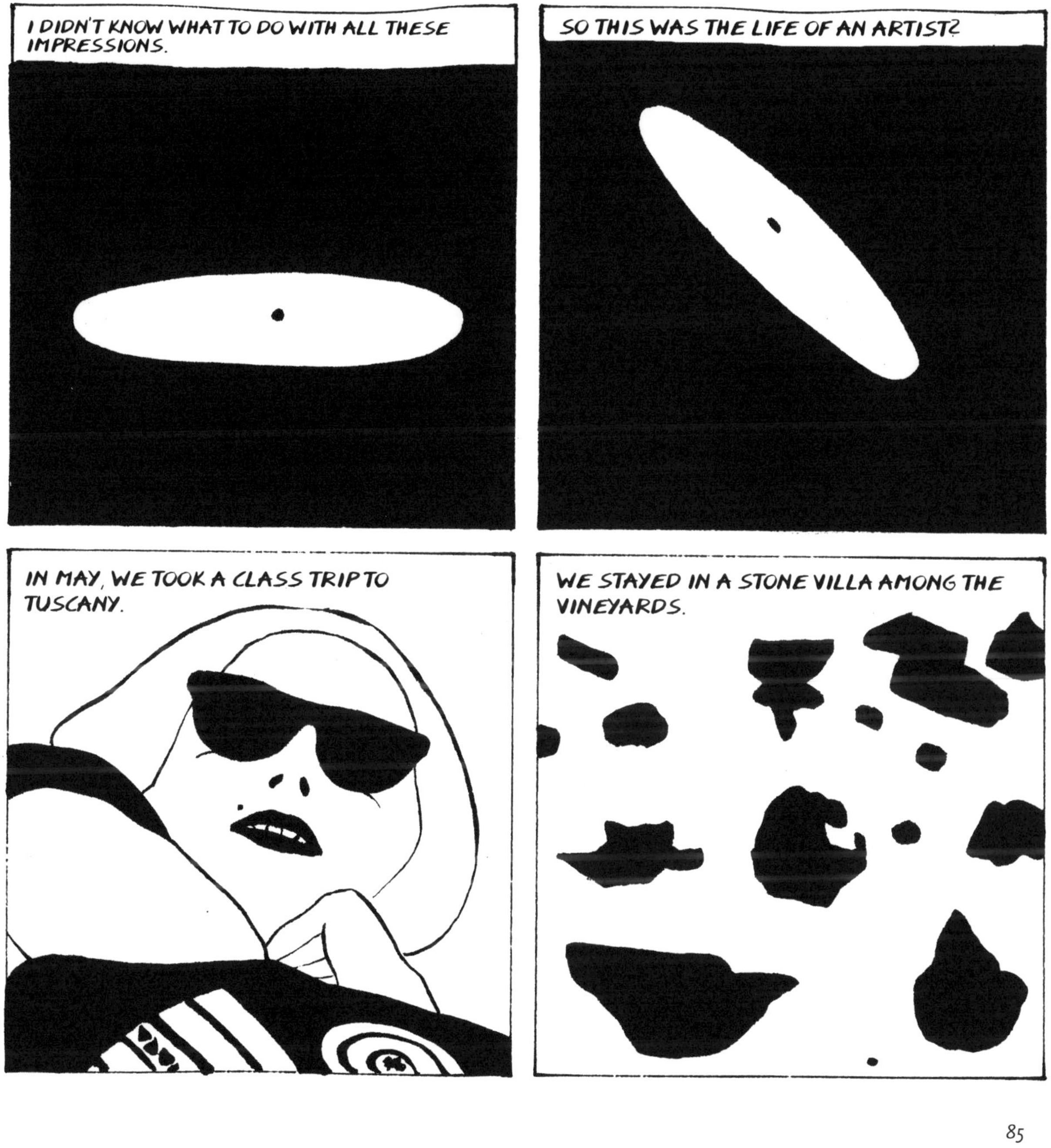
I DIDN'T KNOW WHAT TO DO WITH ALL THESE IMPRESSIONS.
SO THIS WAS THE LIFE OF AN ARTIST?
IN MAY, WE TOOK A CLASS TRIP TO TUSCANY.
WE STAYED IN A STONE VILLA AMONG THE VINEYARDS.

DURING THE DAY, WE DREW.

OR WENT SIGHTSEEING.

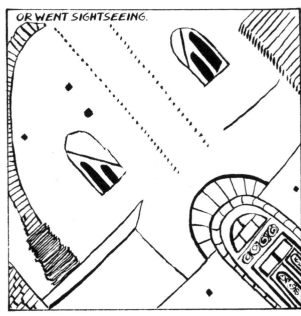

WE DRANK A LOT.

AND SPENT MANY NIGHTS DISCUSSING ART.

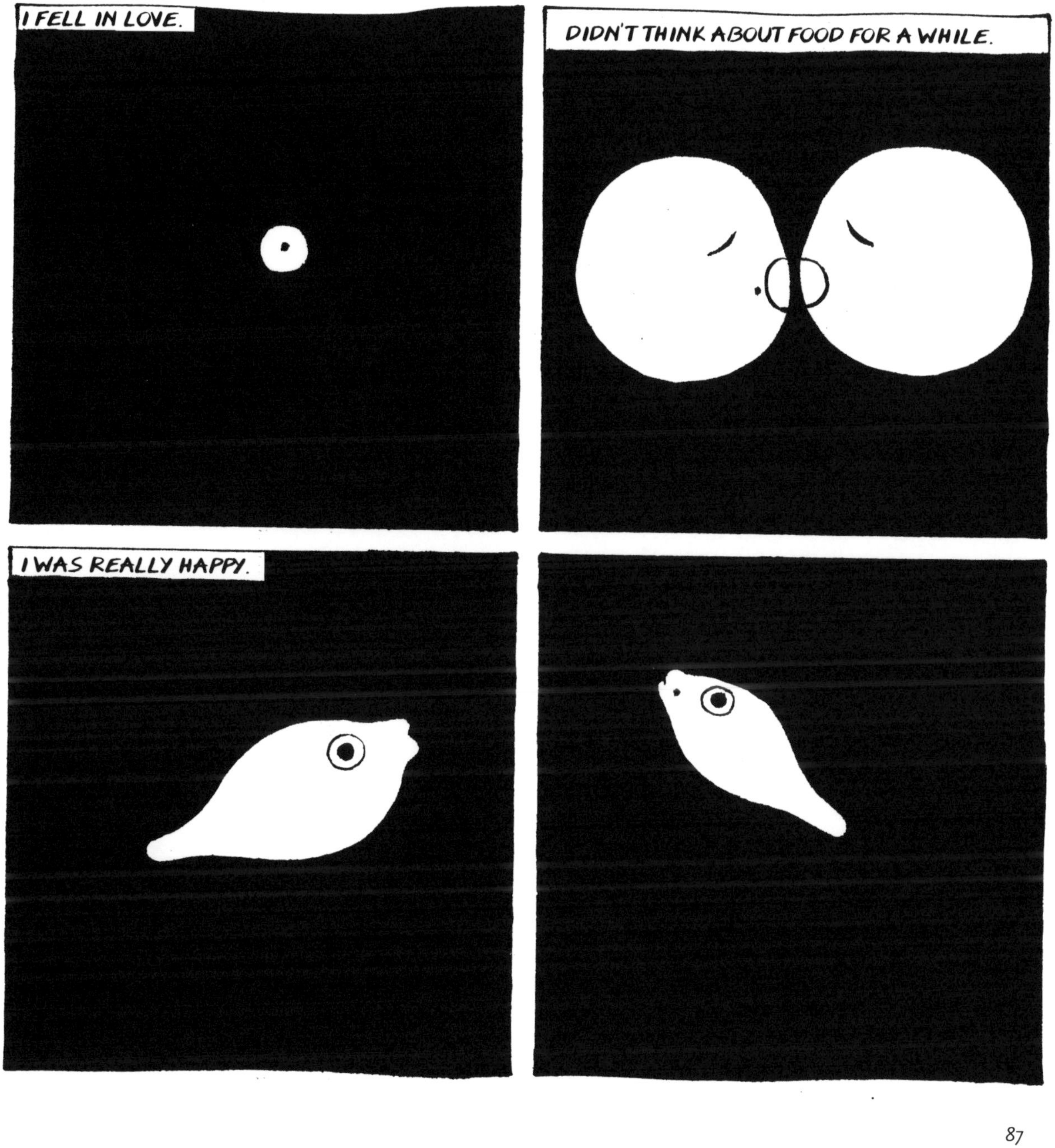
I FELL IN LOVE.
DIDN'T THINK ABOUT FOOD FOR A WHILE.
I WAS REALLY HAPPY.

BACK IN SALZBURG:

I'VE GOT A GIRLFRIEND.

CHAOS.

BUT YOU ARE MY MUSE.

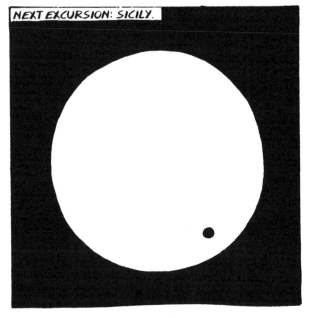

NEXT EXCURSION: SICILY.

LOVESICKNESS.

MAJOR PROBLEMS WITH MY FATHER.

ARTIST LOWLIFES SHOULD ALL BE WIPED OUT.

PLUS MY EATING DISORDER.

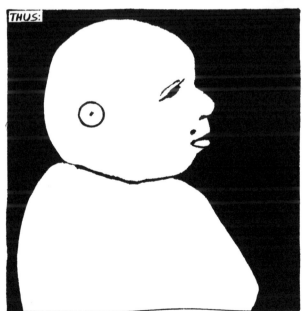

THUS:

NERVOUS BREAKDOWN.

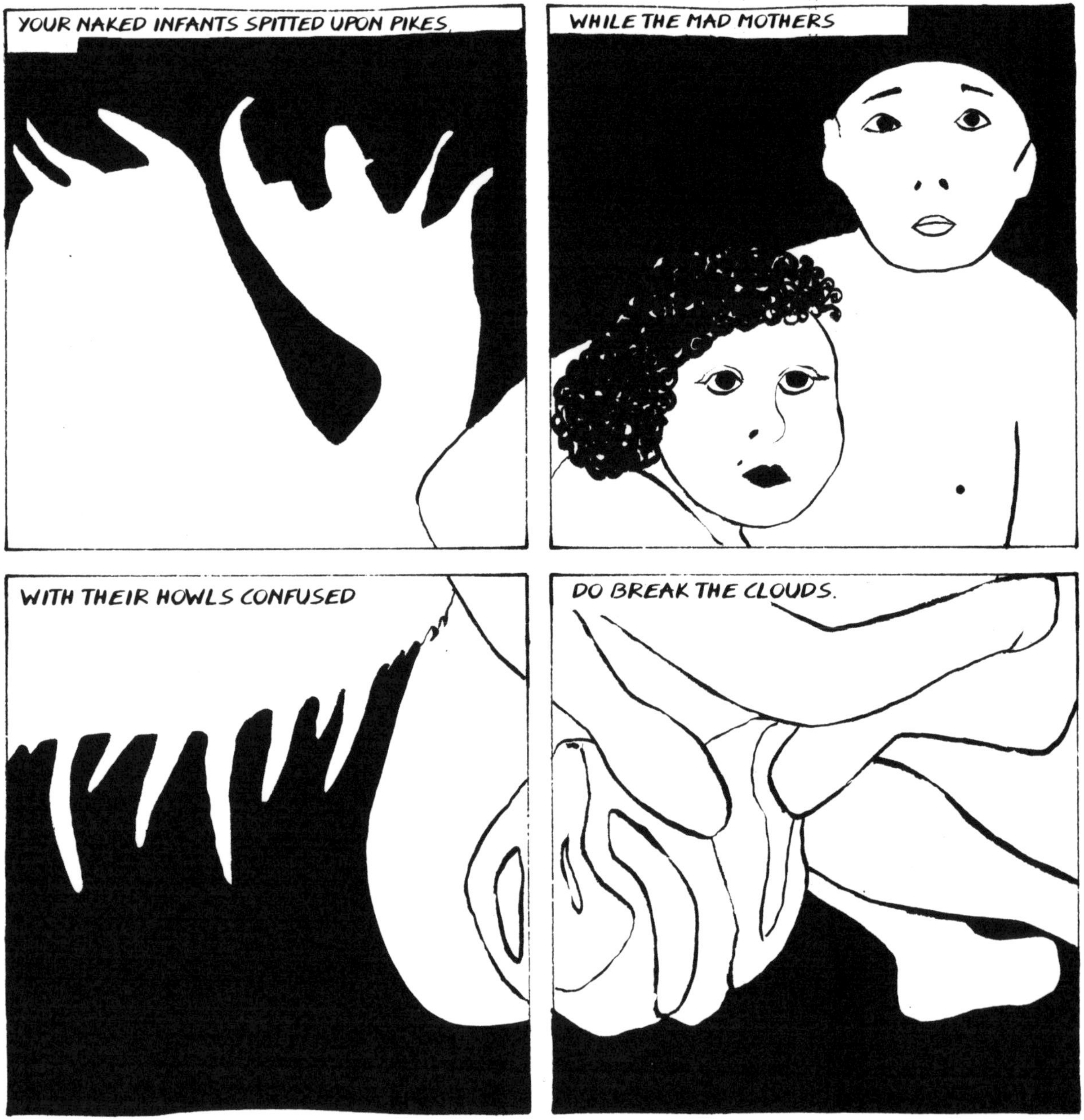
YOUR NAKED INFANTS SPITTED UPON PIKES,
WHILE THE MAD MOTHERS
WITH THEIR HOWLS CONFUSED
DO BREAK THE CLOUDS.

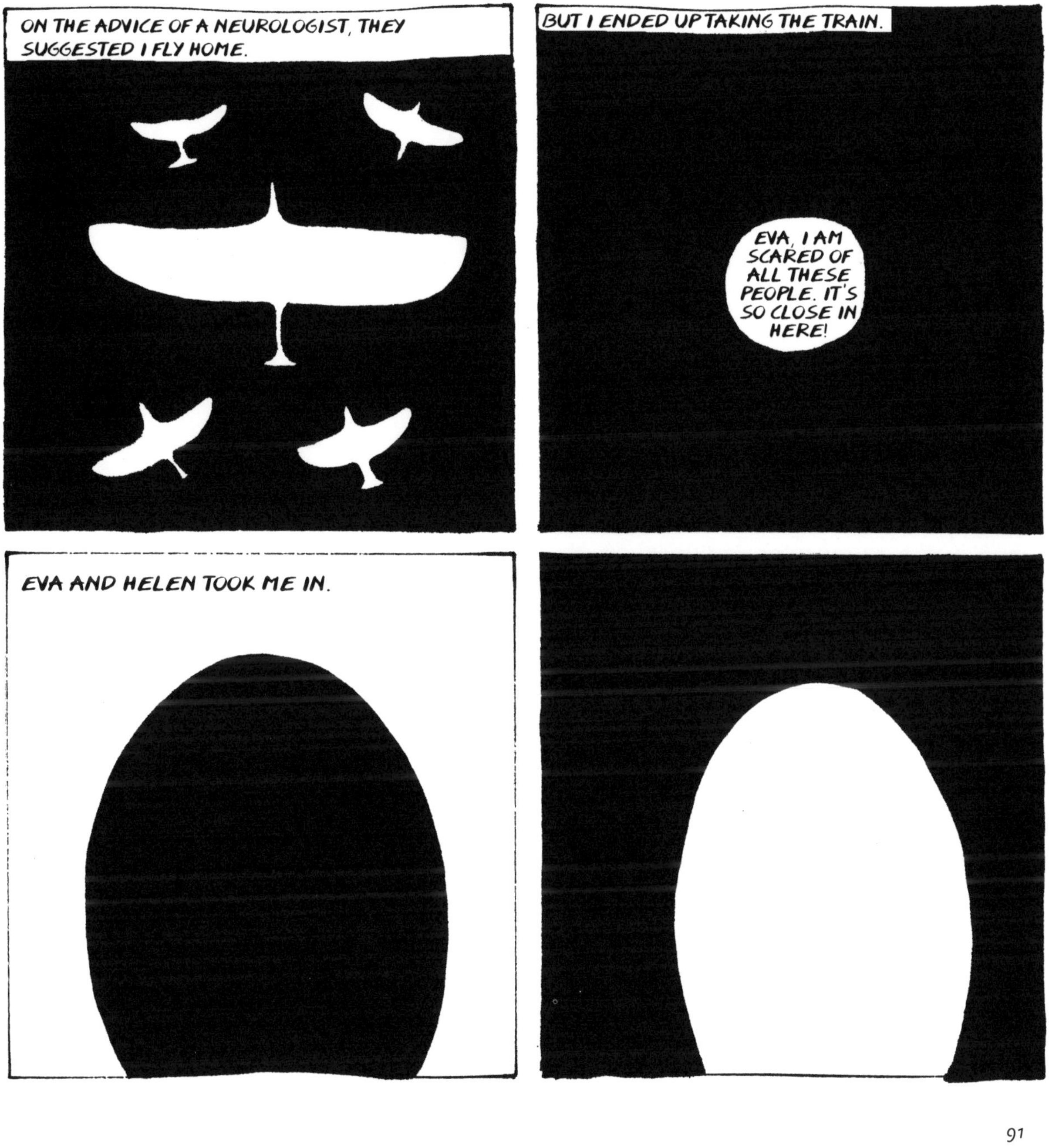
ON THE ADVICE OF A NEUROLOGIST, THEY SUGGESTED I FLY HOME.
BUT I ENDED UP TAKING THE TRAIN.
EVA, I AM SCARED OF ALL THESE PEOPLE. IT'S SO CLOSE IN HERE!
EVA AND HELEN TOOK ME IN.

I SLEPT 36 HOURS.

THEN I HAD TESTS AT THE PSYCHIATRIC CLINIC.

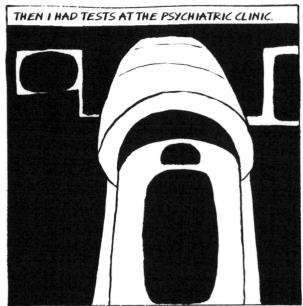

I SHOWED THE DOCTOR THE DRAWINGS I HAD MADE DURING MY NERVOUS BREAKDOWN.

HE WANTED TO ADMIT ME AS AN IN-PATIENT.

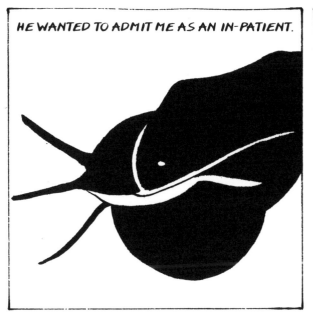

AND TALKED ABOUT ANESTHESIA.

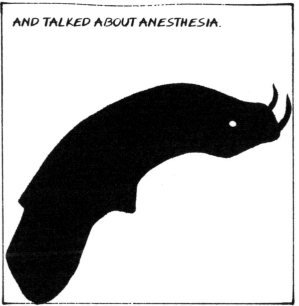

EVA STOPPED ME FROM AGREEING TO THAT.

I MET WITH OTHER DOCTORS.

1. DIAGNOSIS: INCURABLE ILLNESS (MRI)

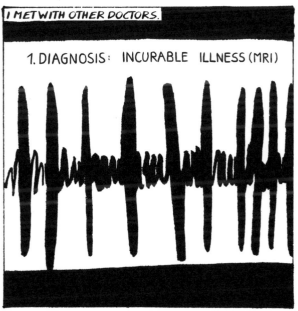

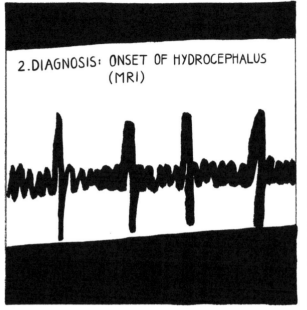

2. DIAGNOSIS: ONSET OF HYDROCEPHALUS (MRI)

3. DIAGNOSIS: BUMPED HER HEAD AS A CHILD (SCAR).
OTHER THAN THAT, NOTHING'S WRONG WITH YOU.

I DROVE HOME TO MY PARENTS AND TOLD THEM EVERYTHING.

MOM, DAD!
I SAW
MONSTERS!

MY MOTHER WAS WORRIED SICK.

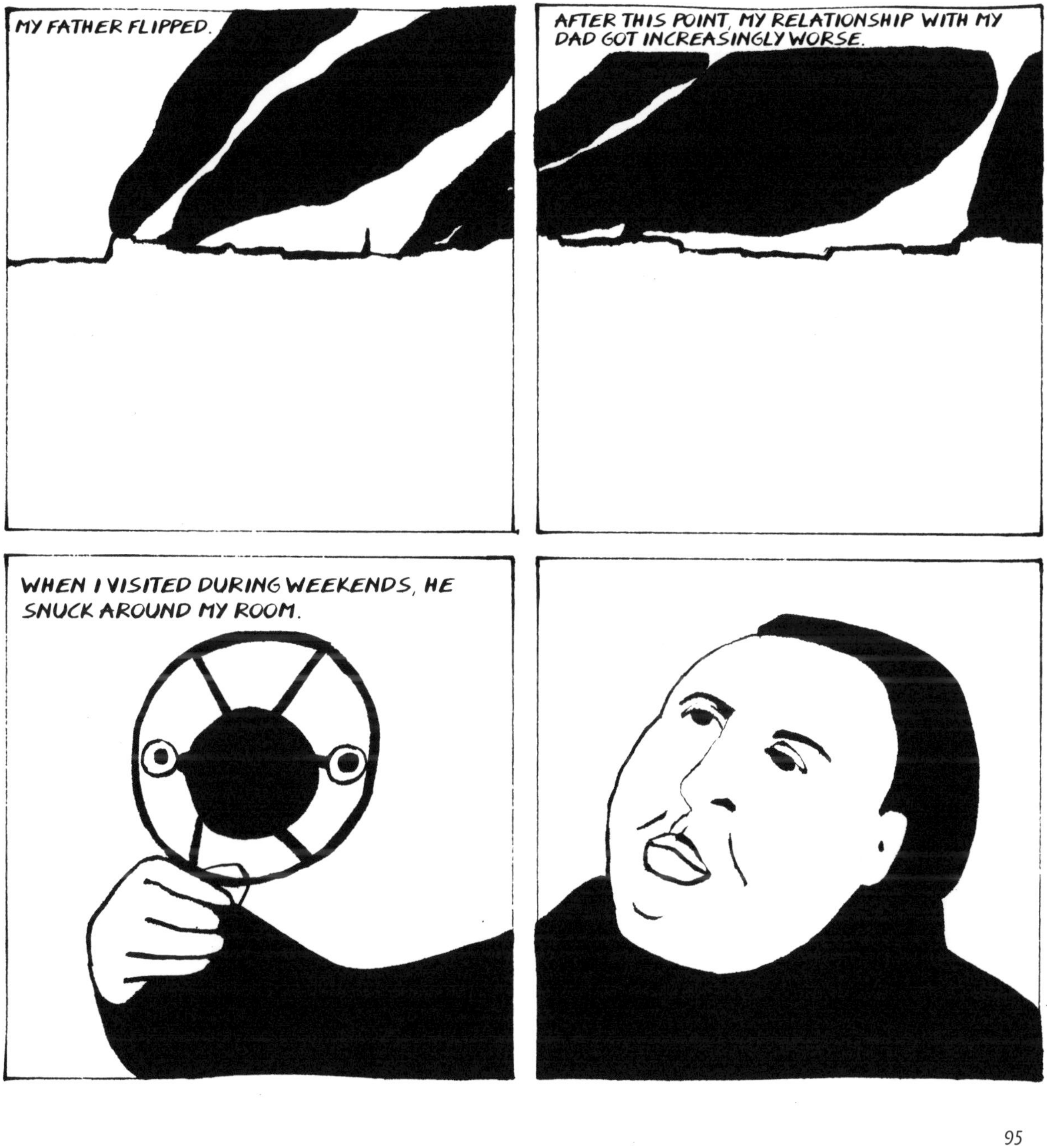
MY FATHER FLIPPED.
AFTER THIS POINT, MY RELATIONSHIP WITH MY DAD GOT INCREASINGLY WORSE.
WHEN I VISITED DURING WEEKENDS, HE SNUCK AROUND MY ROOM.

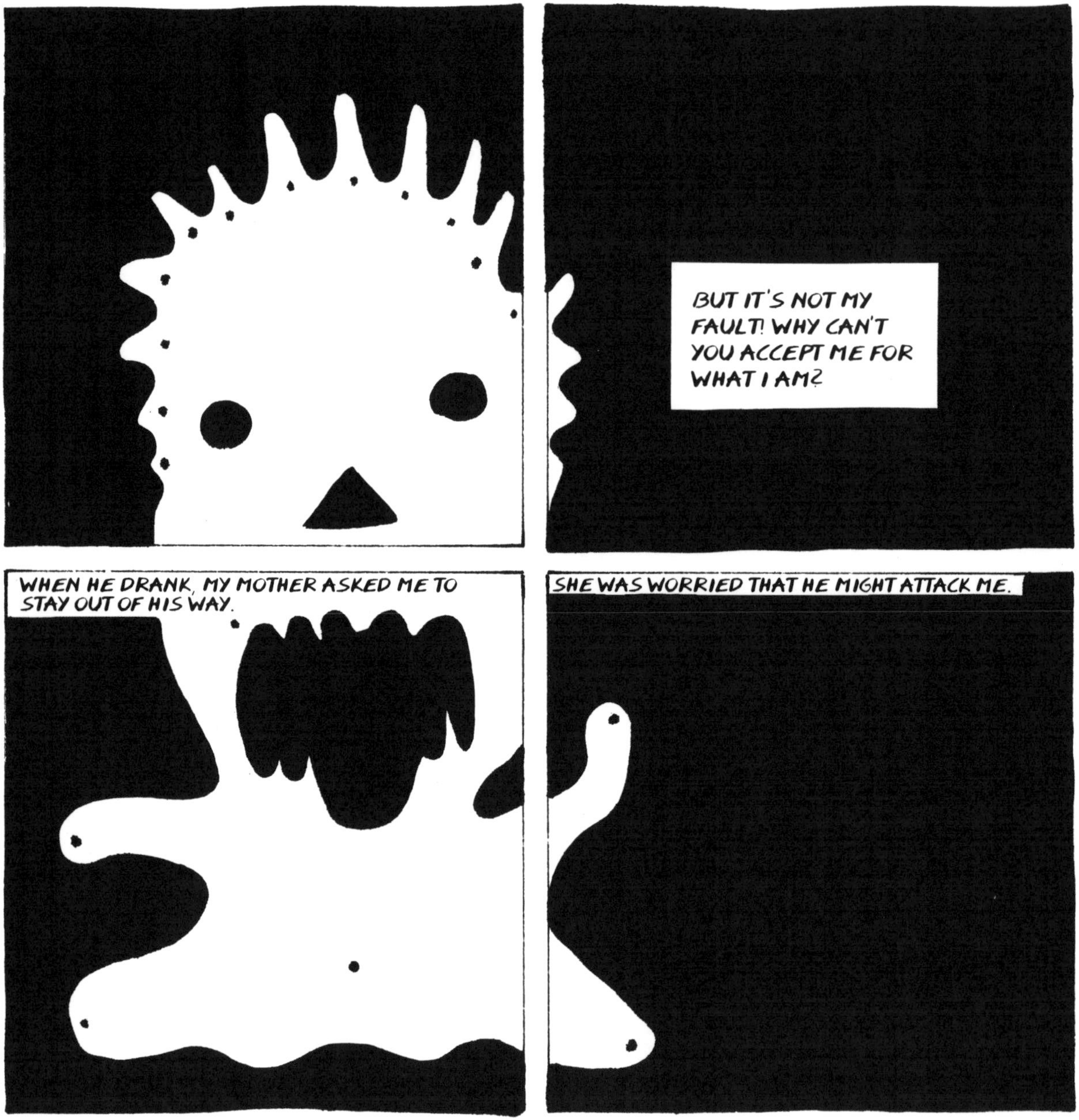
BUT IT'S NOT MY FAULT! WHY CAN'T YOU ACCEPT ME FOR WHAT I AM?
WHEN HE DRANK, MY MOTHER ASKED ME TO STAY OUT OF HIS WAY.
SHE WAS WORRIED THAT HE MIGHT ATTACK ME.

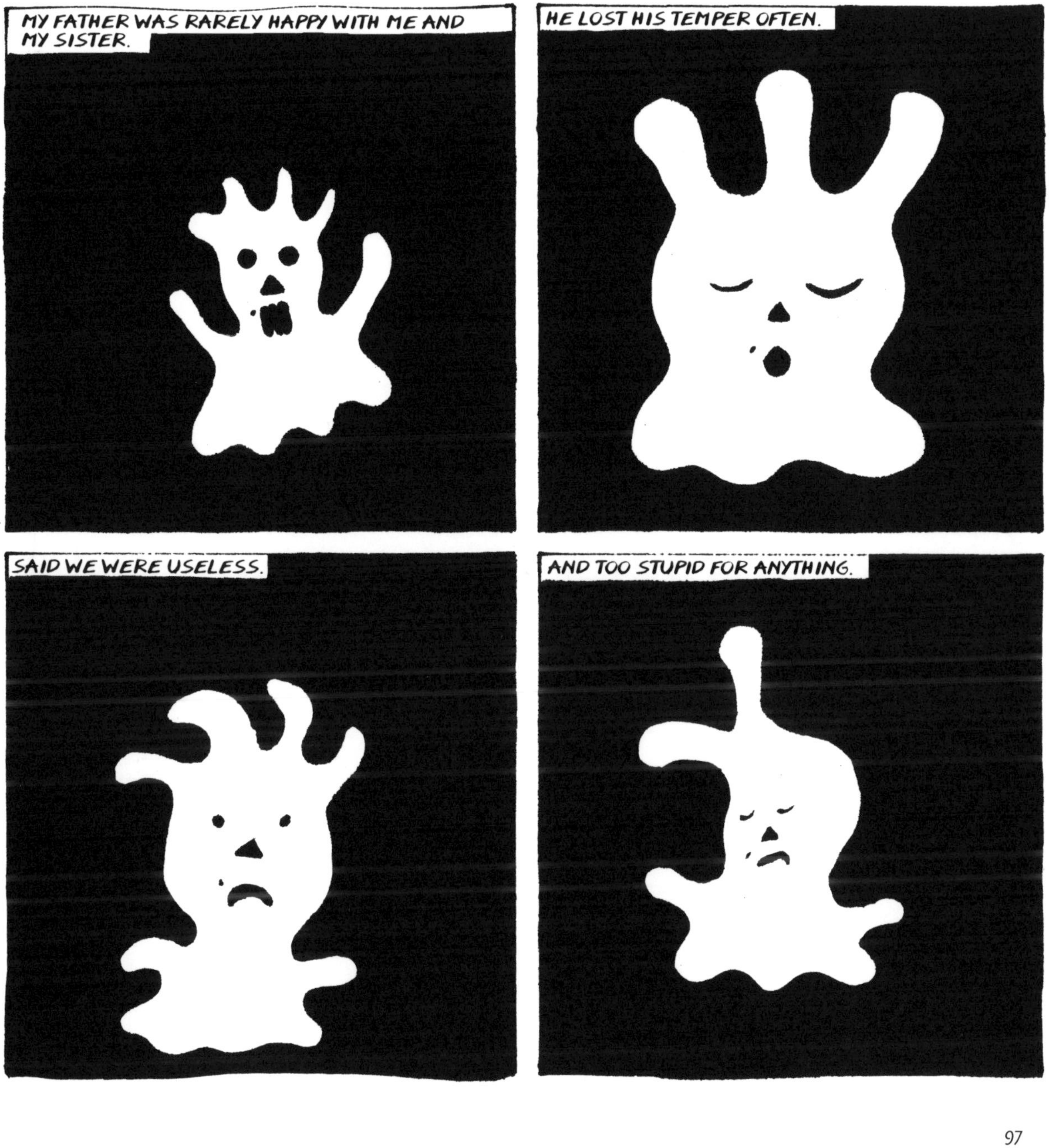
MY FATHER WAS RARELY HAPPY WITH ME AND MY SISTER.
HE LOST HIS TEMPER OFTEN.
SAID WE WERE USELESS.
AND TOO STUPID FOR ANYTHING.

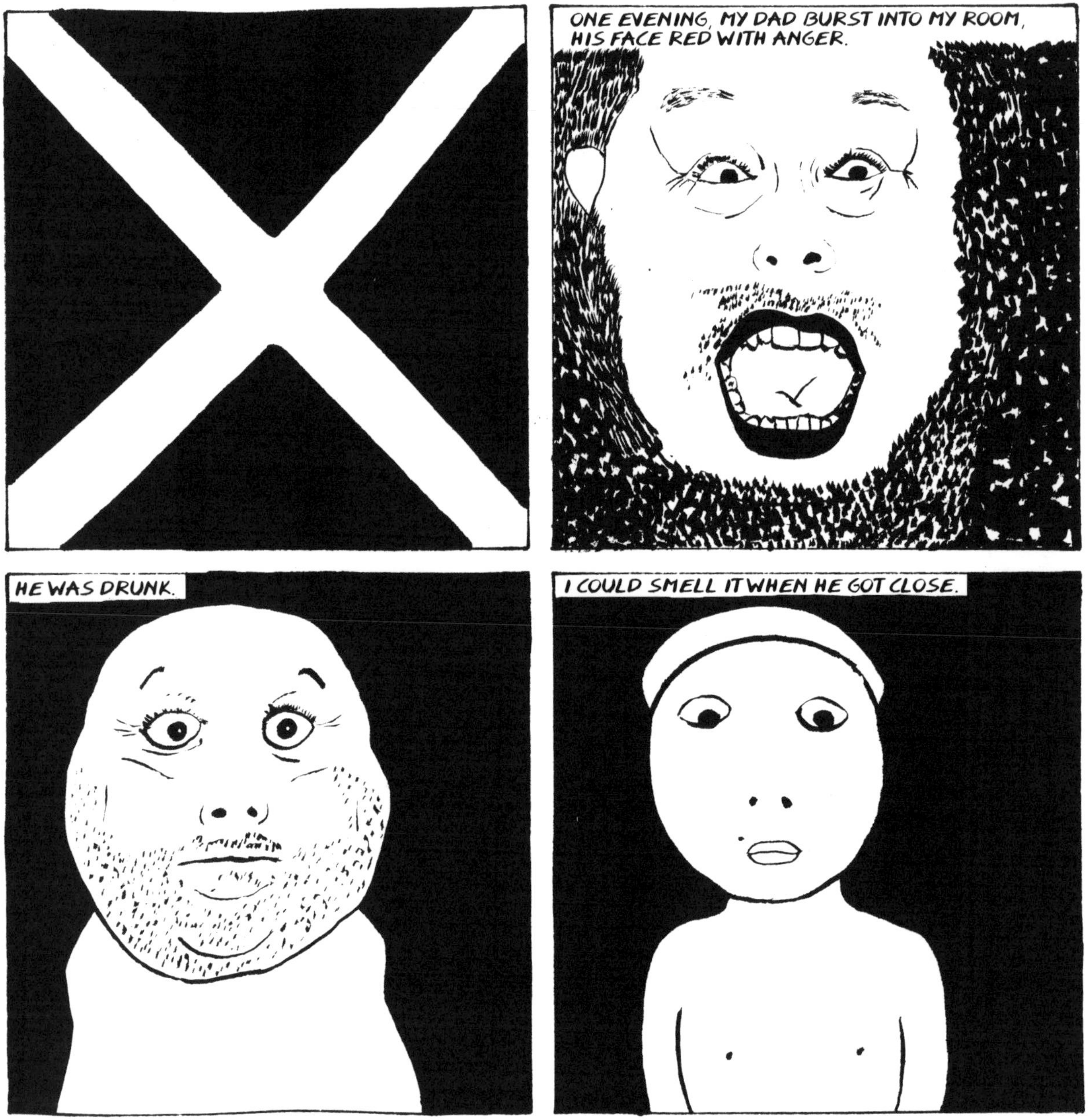
ONE EVENING, MY DAD BURST INTO MY ROOM, HIS FACE RED WITH ANGER.
HE WAS DRUNK.
I COULD SMELL IT WHEN HE GOT CLOSE.

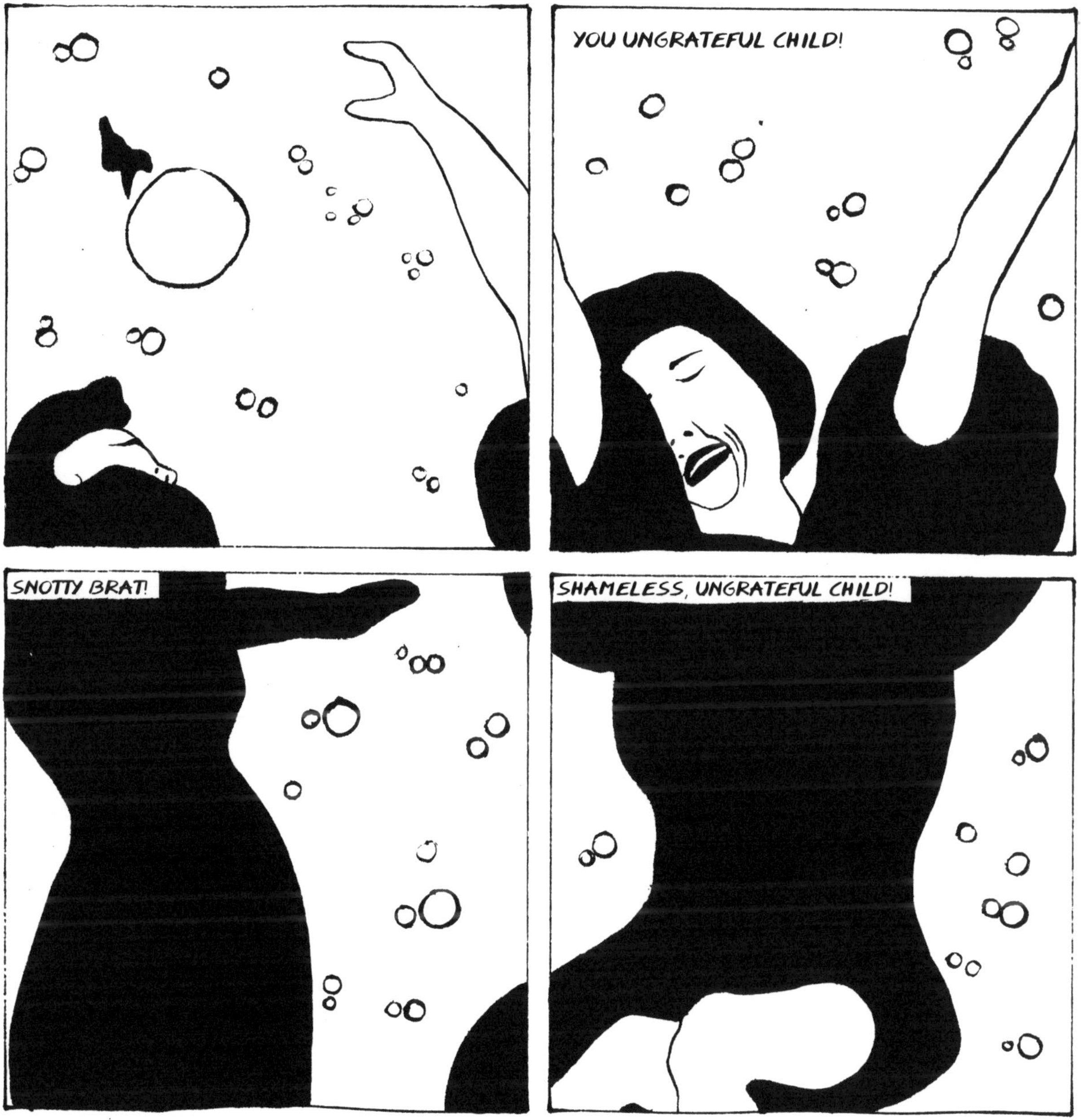
YOU UNGRATEFUL CHILD!
SNOTTY BRAT!
SHAMELESS, UNGRATEFUL CHILD!

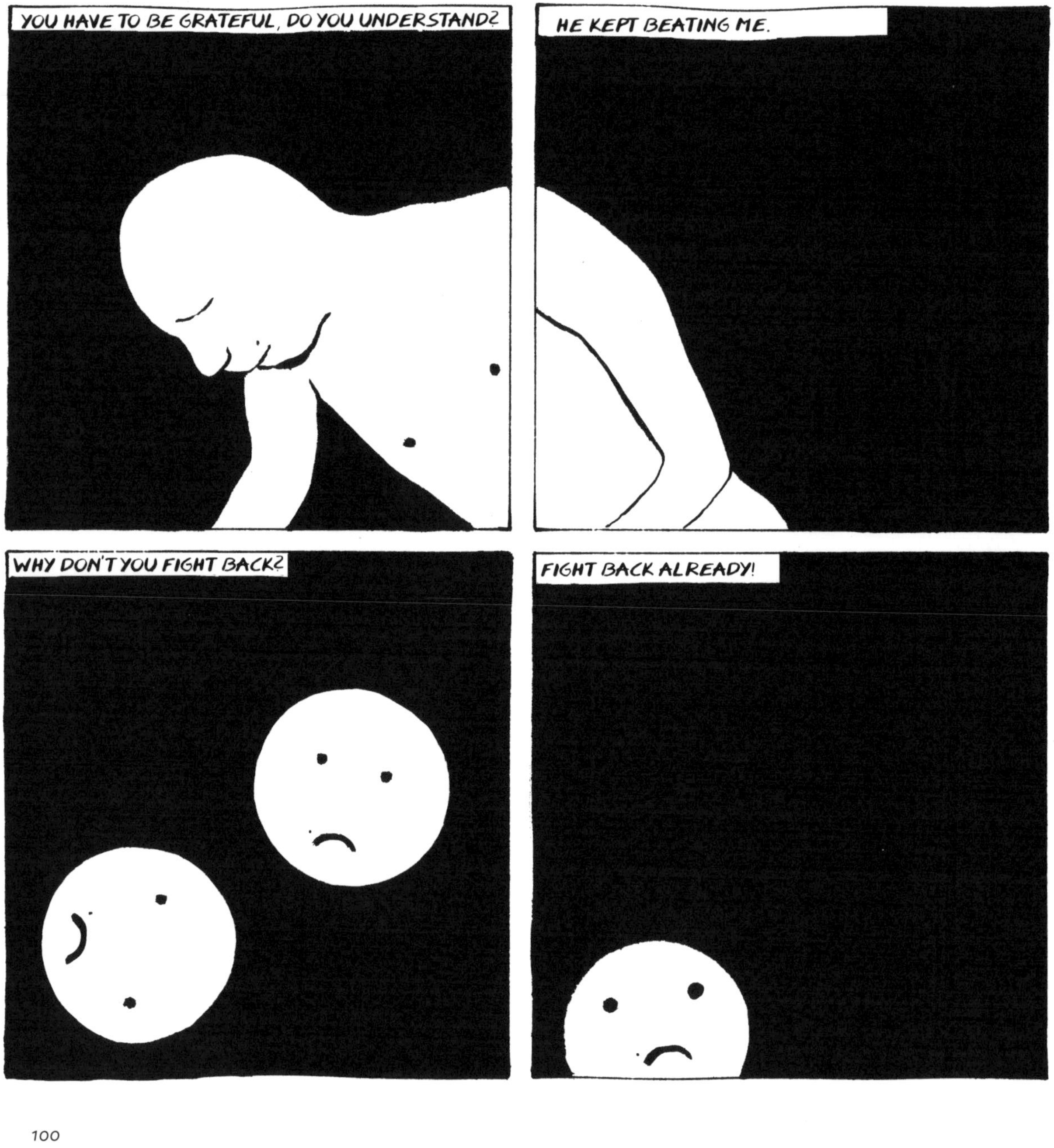
YOU HAVE TO BE GRATEFUL, DO YOU UNDERSTAND?
HE KEPT BEATING ME.
WHY DON'T YOU FIGHT BACK?
FIGHT BACK ALREADY!

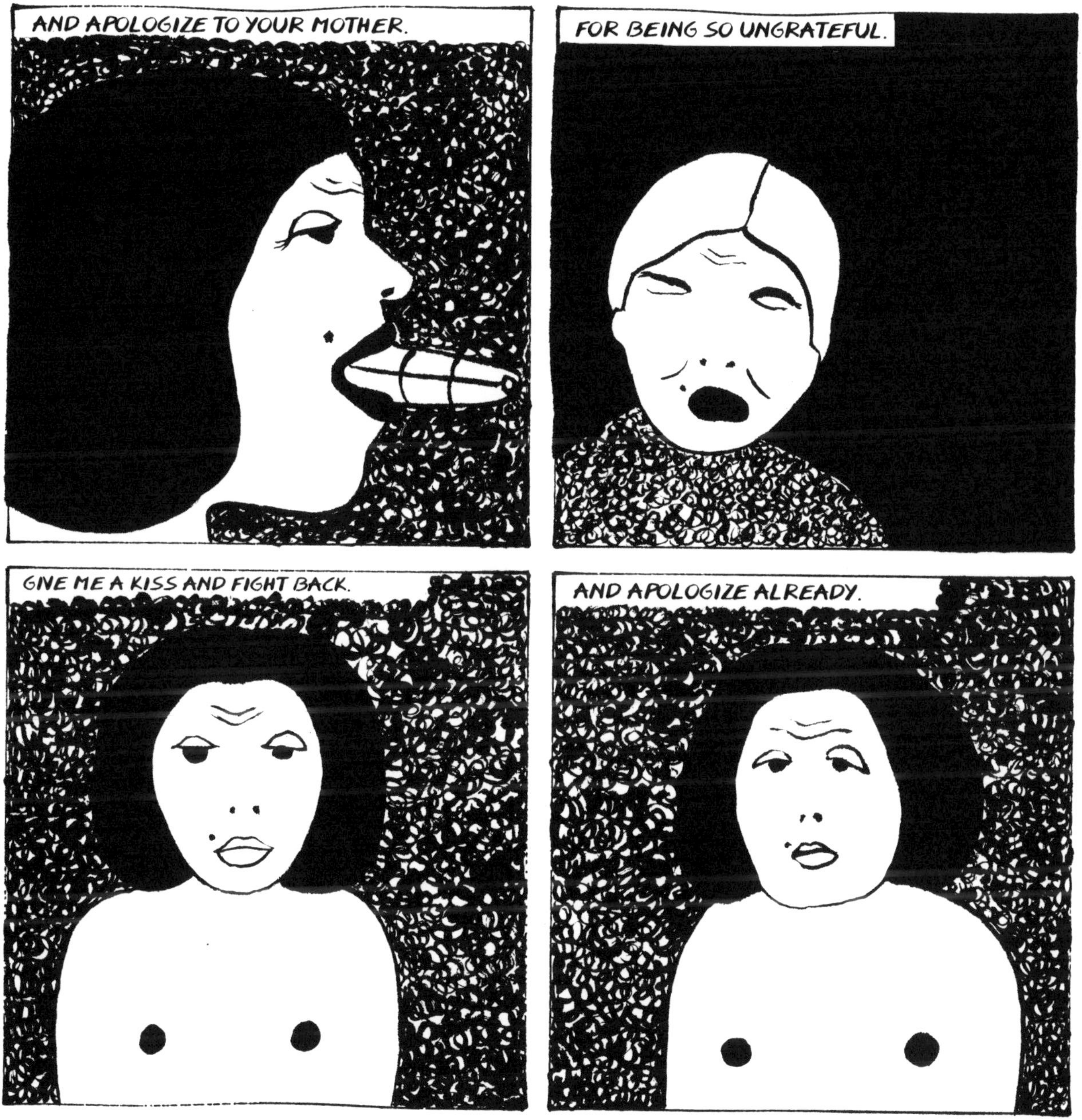
AND APOLOGIZE TO YOUR MOTHER.
FOR BEING SO UNGRATEFUL.
GIVE ME A KISS AND FIGHT BACK.
AND APOLOGIZE ALREADY.

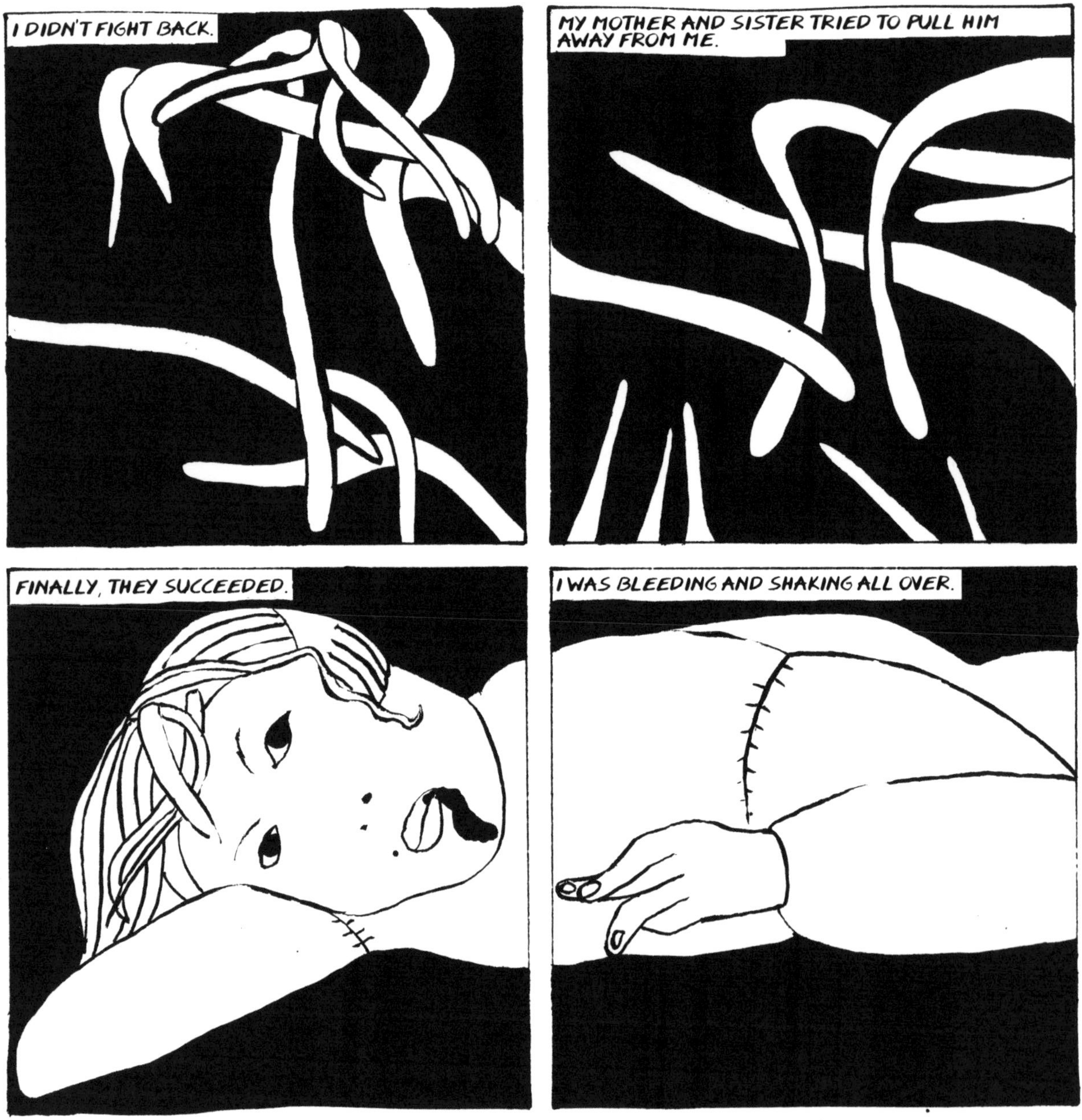
I DIDN'T FIGHT BACK.
MY MOTHER AND SISTER TRIED TO PULL HIM AWAY FROM ME.
FINALLY, THEY SUCCEEDED.
I WAS BLEEDING AND SHAKING ALL OVER.

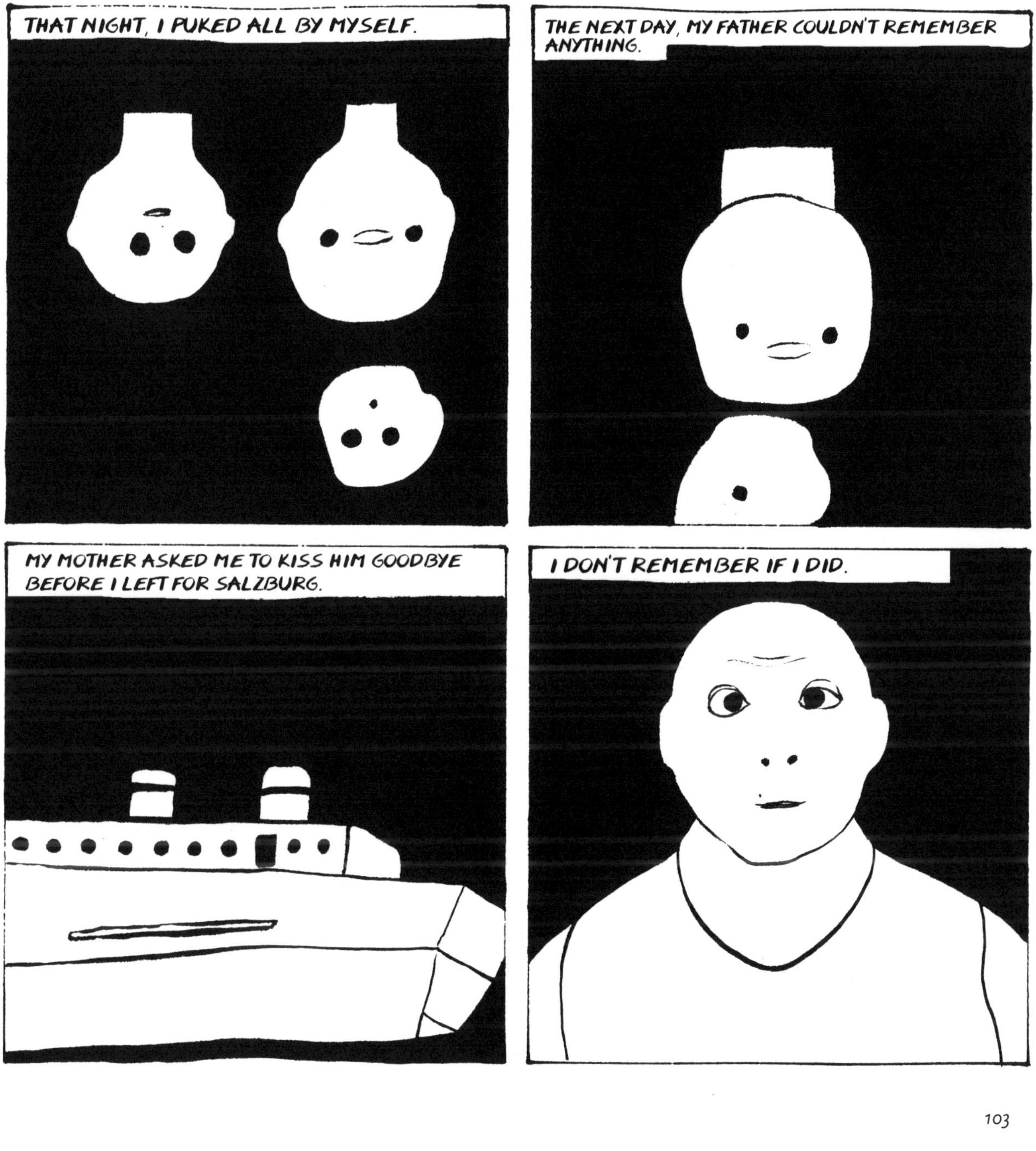
THAT NIGHT, I PUKED ALL BY MYSELF.
THE NEXT DAY, MY FATHER COULDN'T REMEMBER ANYTHING.
MY MOTHER ASKED ME TO KISS HIM GOODBYE BEFORE I LEFT FOR SALZBURG.
I DON'T REMEMBER IF I DID.

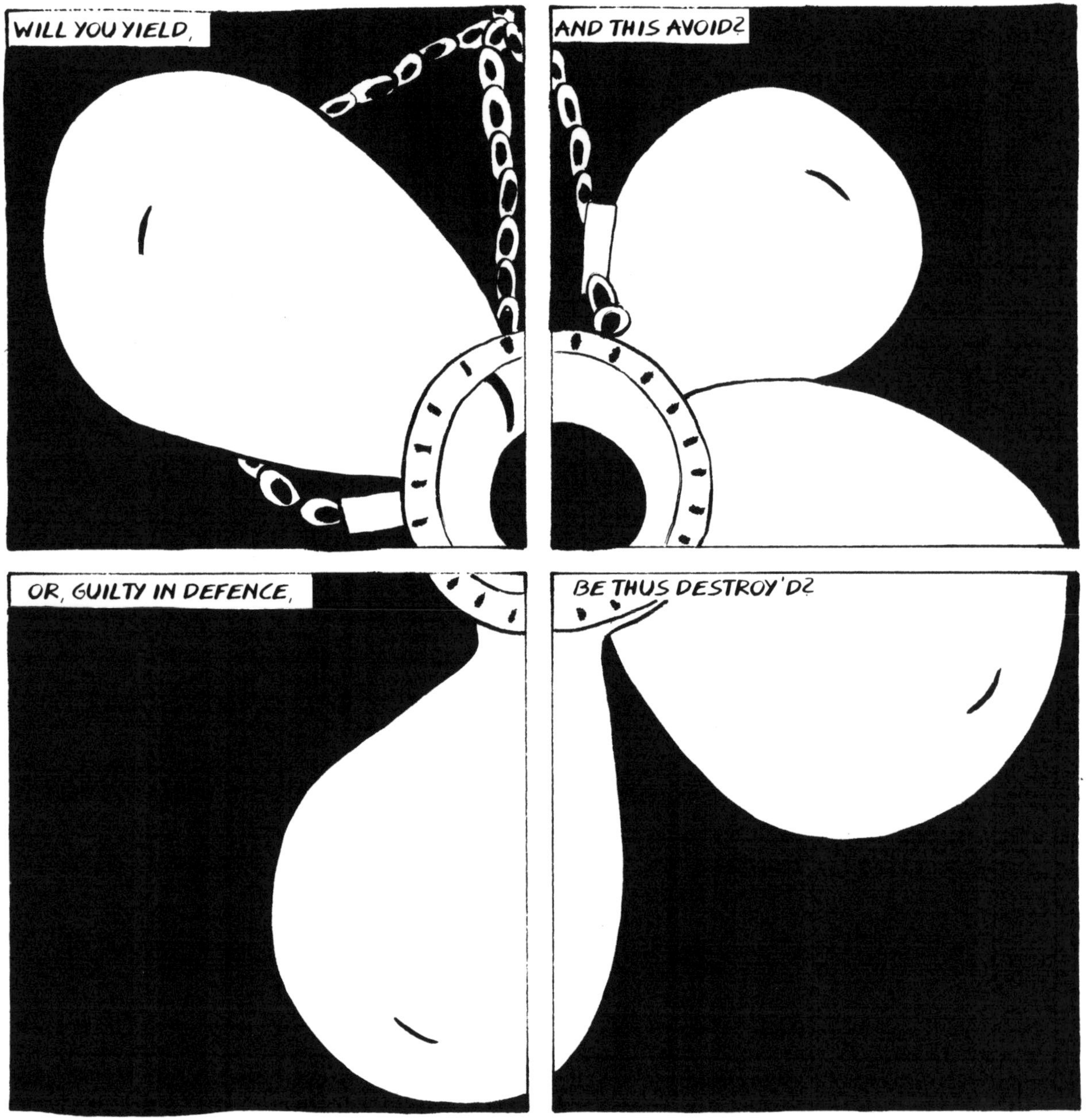

WILL YOU YIELD,
AND THIS AVOID?
OR, GUILTY IN DEFENCE,
BE THUS DESTROY'D?

I WAS NOW LIVING IN A 50 SQ. FT. APARTMENT IN MÖNCHSBERG.

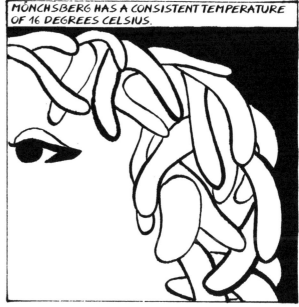

MÖNCHSBERG HAS A CONSISTENT TEMPERATURE OF 16 DEGREES CELSIUS.

IT IS SOMEWHAT THREATENING, HEAVY ...

... TO LIVE THAT CLOSE TO THE MOUNTAIN.

EVERYTHING BECAME MORE HOPELESS FOR ME.

MY SELF-DESTRUCTIVE COMPULSION WAS FULLY IGNITED AGAIN.

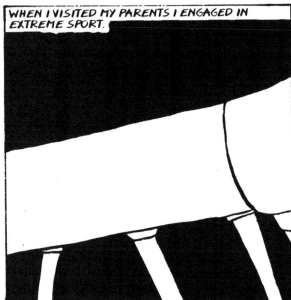

WHEN I VISITED MY PARENTS I ENGAGED IN EXTREME SPORT.

WORKED OUT ON THE EXERCISE MACHINE AT 3 IN THE MORNING.

... HAD BINGE ATTACKS ...

... THEN WORKED OUT AGAIN ON THE HIGHEST LEVEL.

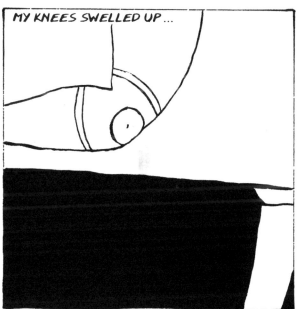

MY KNEES SWELLED UP ...

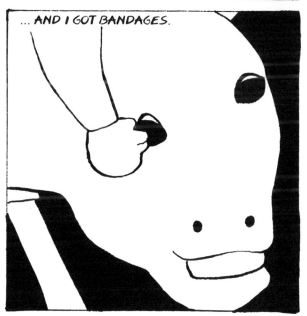

... AND I GOT BANDAGES.

I DIRECTED ALL MY ANGER AT MYSELF.

HAD SUICIDAL THOUGHTS...

... BUT I KNEW I WASN'T CAPABLE.

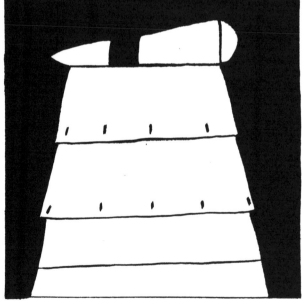

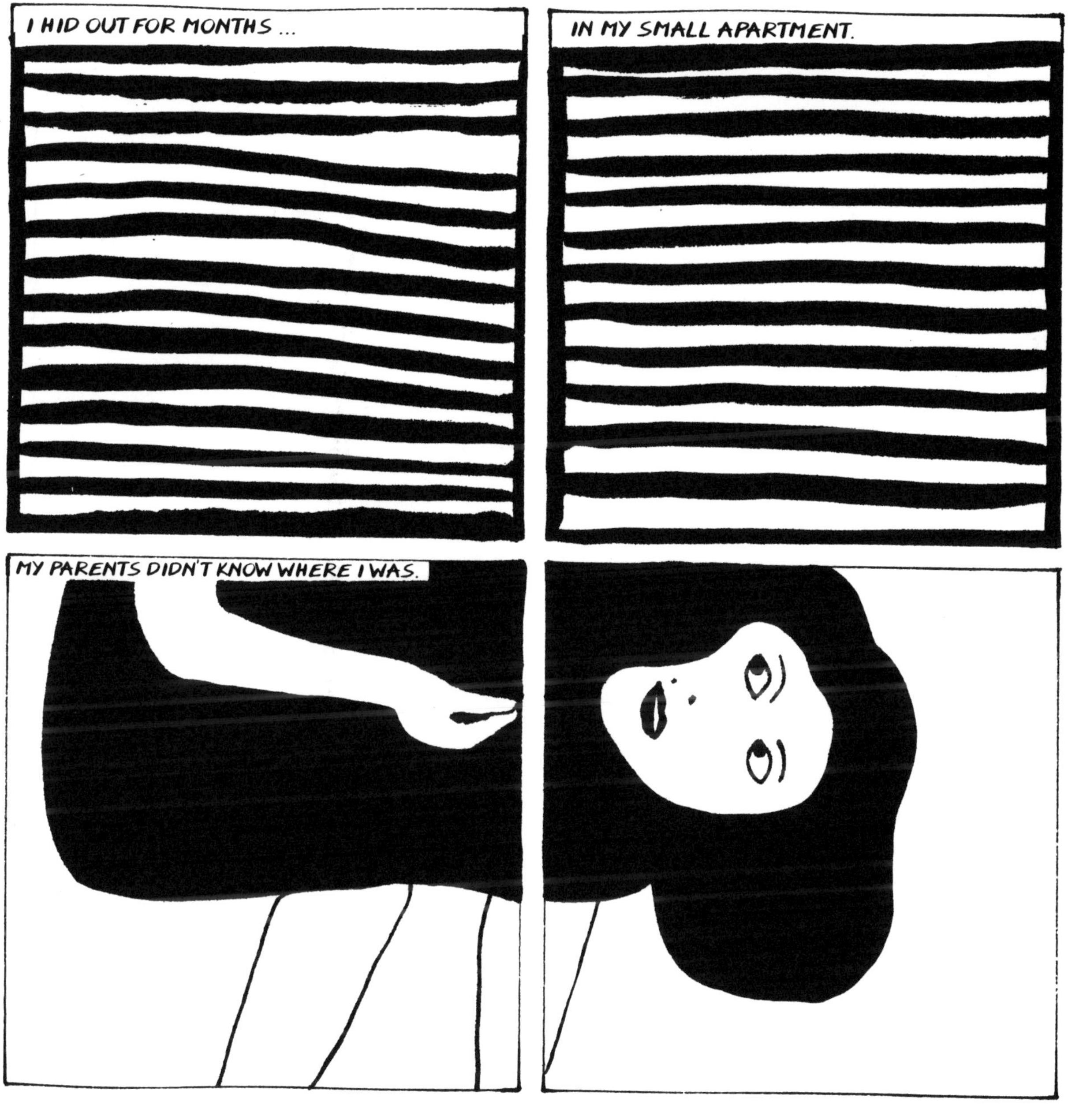
I HID OUT FOR MONTHS ...
IN MY SMALL APARTMENT.
MY PARENTS DIDN'T KNOW WHERE I WAS.

I DIDN'T ANSWER THE PHONE...

DIDN'T PAY MY BILLS...

GOT AN ABSCESSED TOOTH...

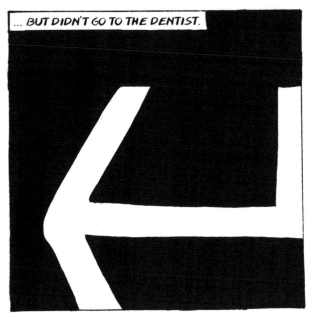

... BUT DIDN'T GO TO THE DENTIST.

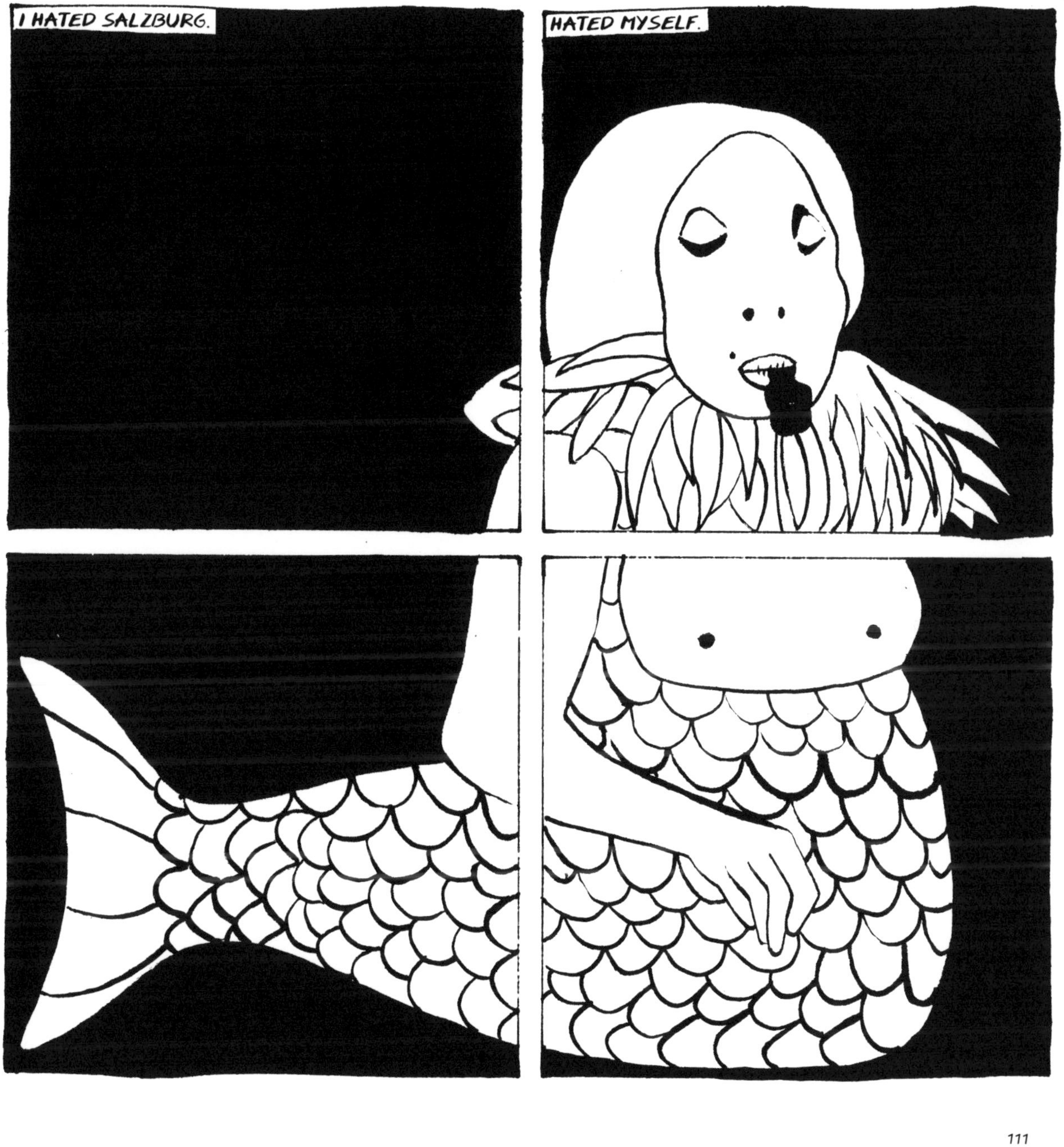
I HATED SALZBURG.
HATED MYSELF.

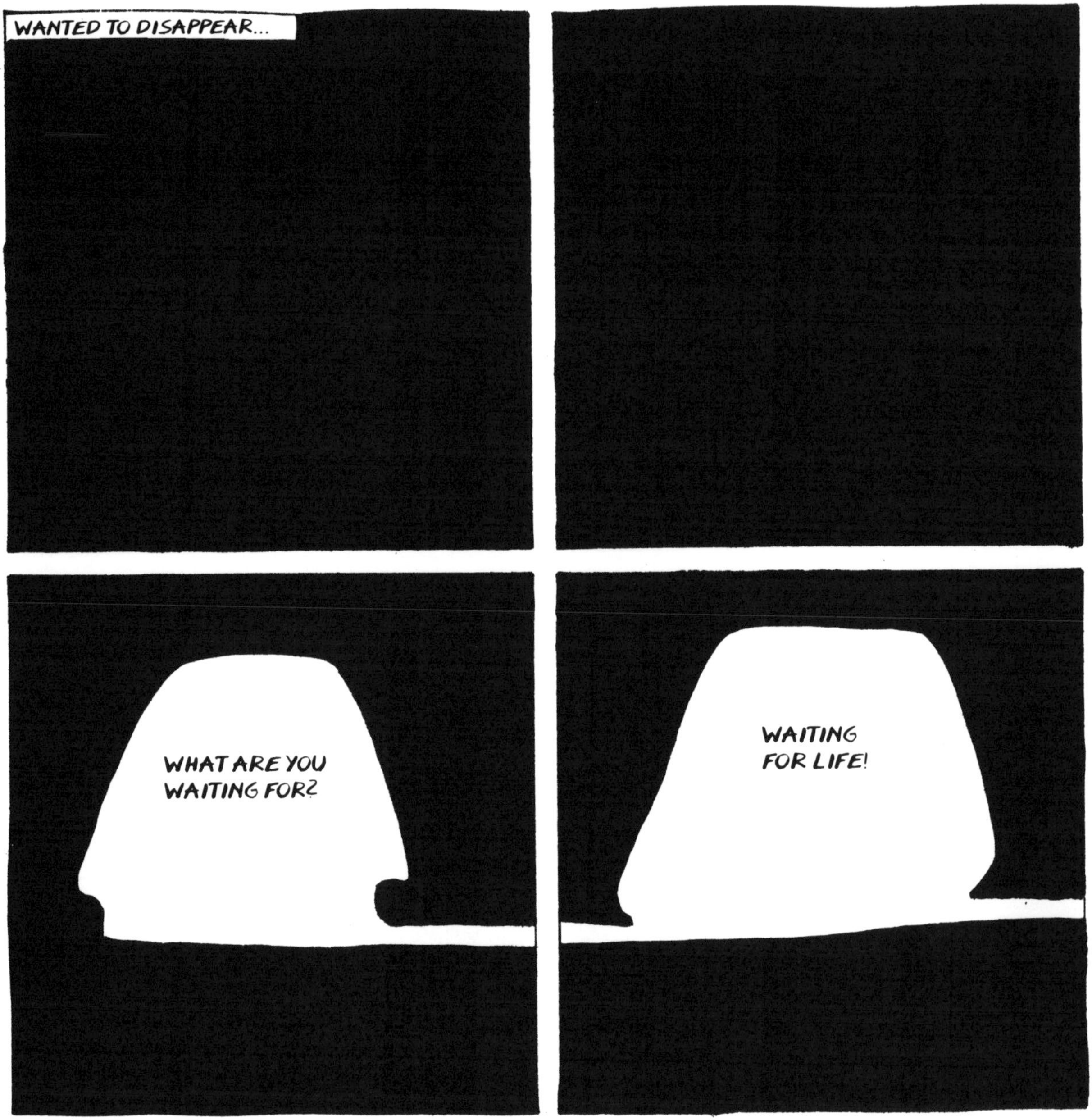
WANTED TO DISAPPEAR...
WHAT ARE YOU WAITING FOR?
WAITING FOR LIFE!

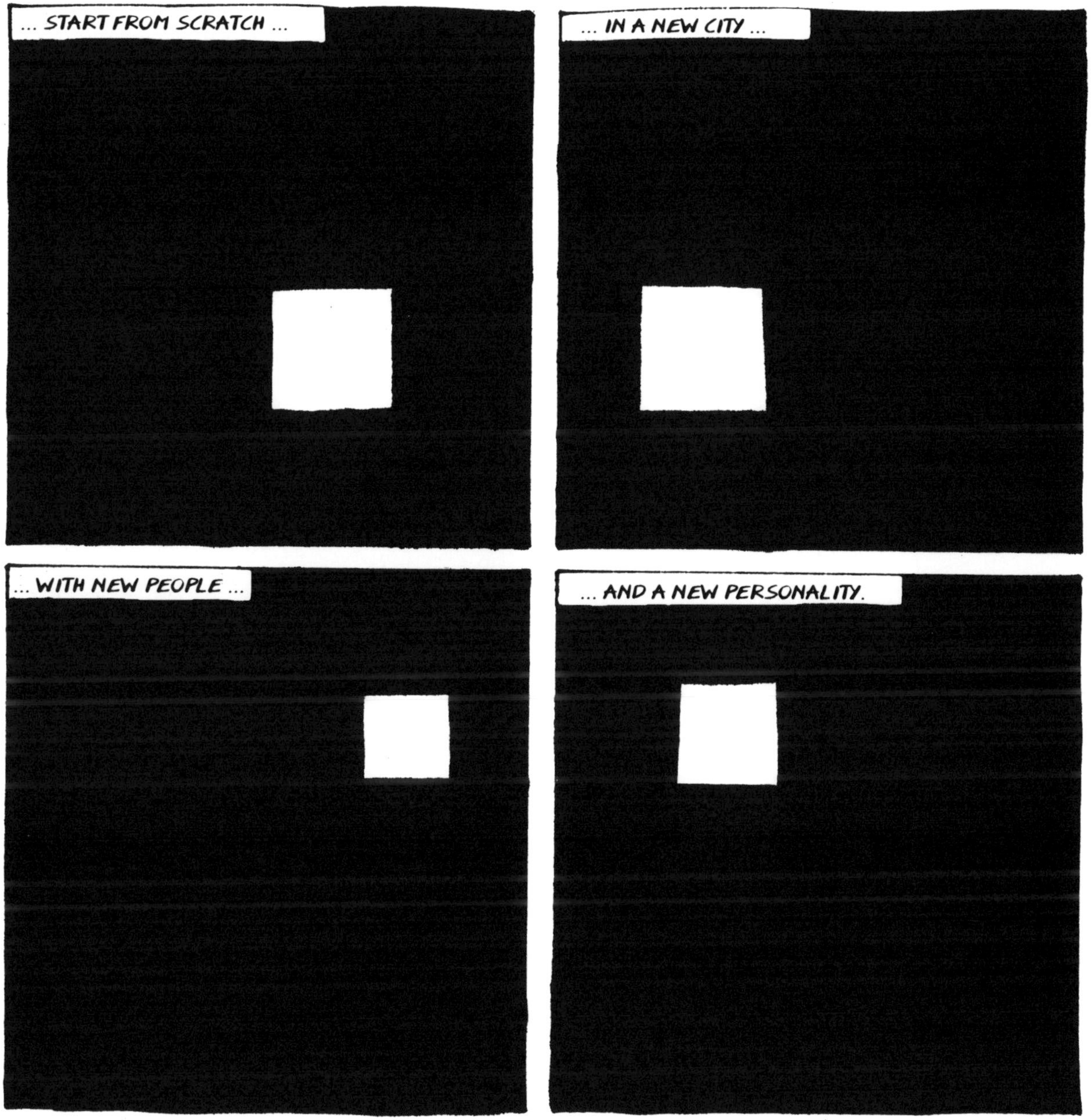
... START FROM SCRATCH ...
... IN A NEW CITY ...
... WITH NEW PEOPLE ...
... AND A NEW PERSONALITY.

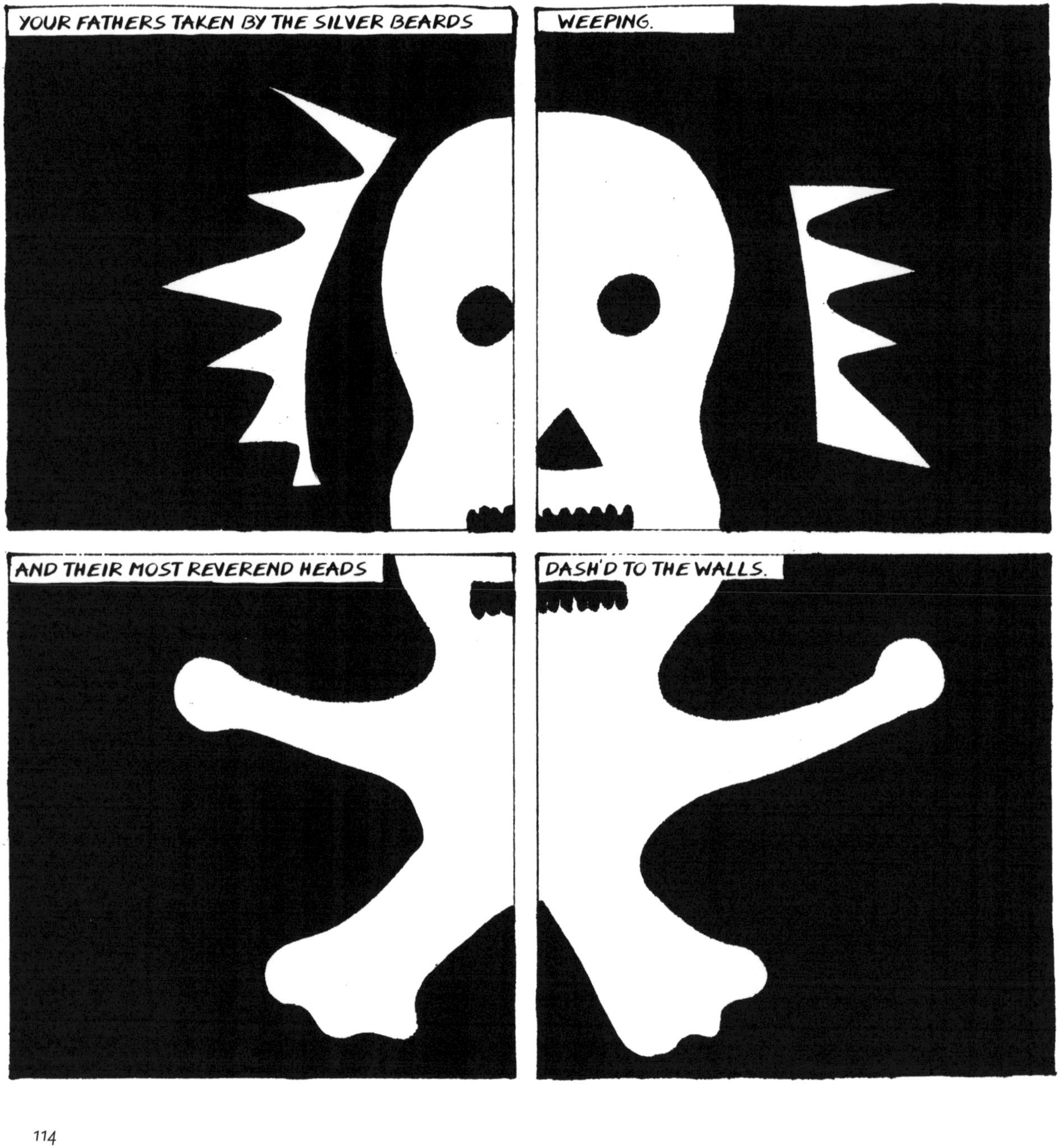
YOUR FATHERS TAKEN BY THE SILVER BEARDS
WEEPING.
AND THEIR MOST REVEREND HEADS
DASH'D TO THE WALLS.

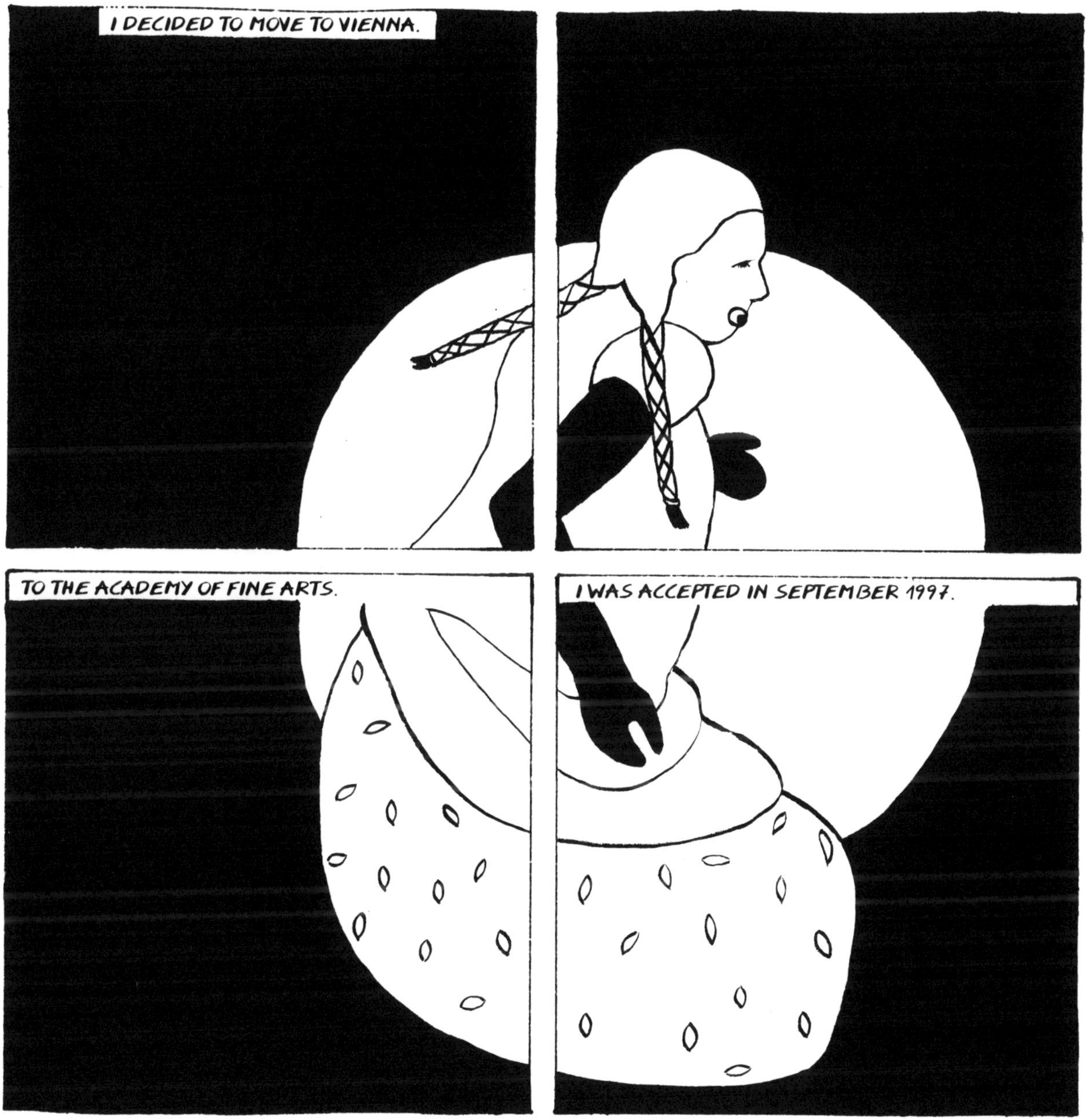
I DECIDED TO MOVE TO VIENNA.
TO THE ACADEMY OF FINE ARTS.
I WAS ACCEPTED IN SEPTEMBER 1997.

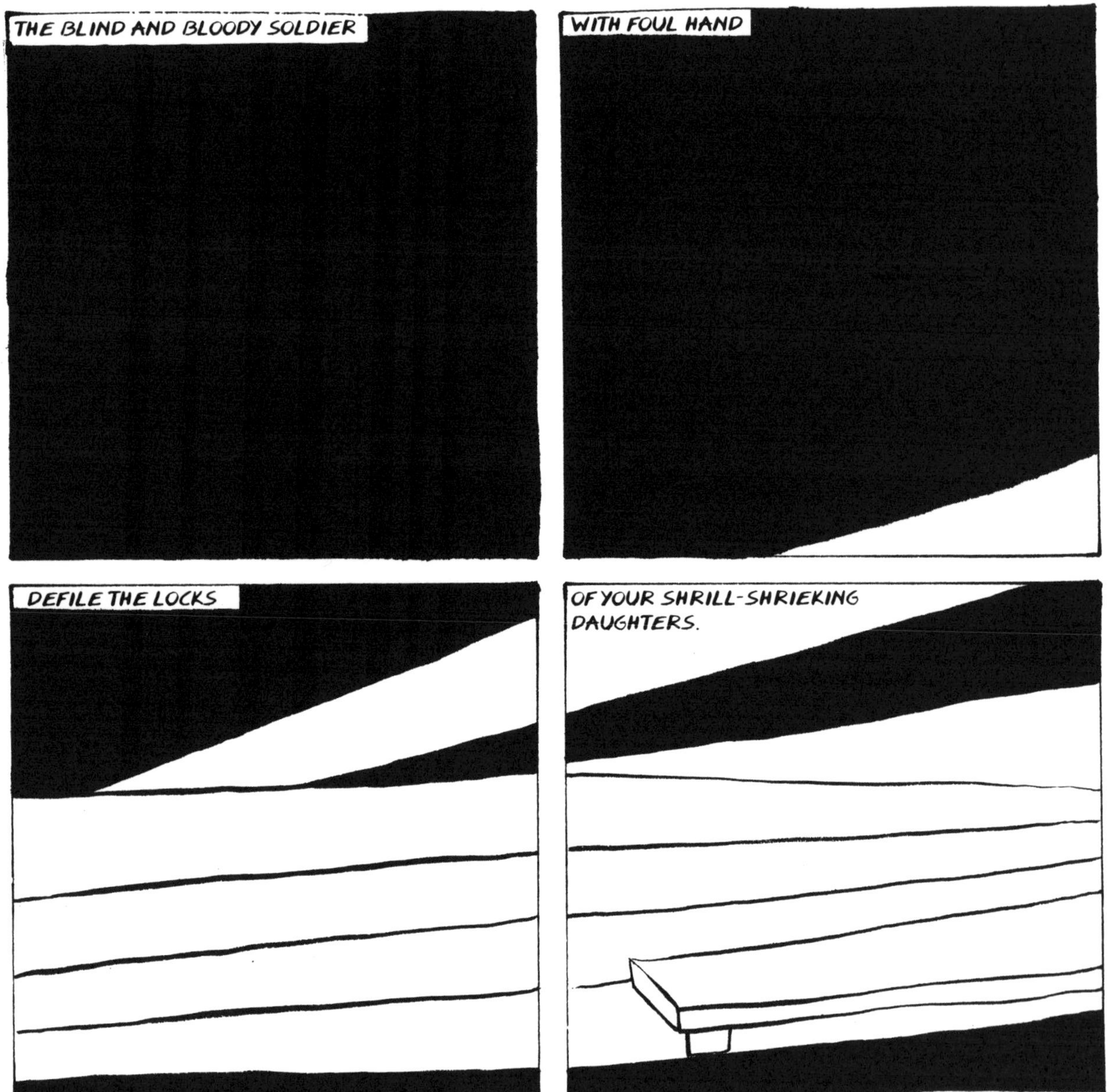
THE BLIND AND BLOODY SOLDIER
WITH FOUL HAND
DEFILE THE LOCKS
OF YOUR SHRILL-SHRIEKING DAUGHTERS.

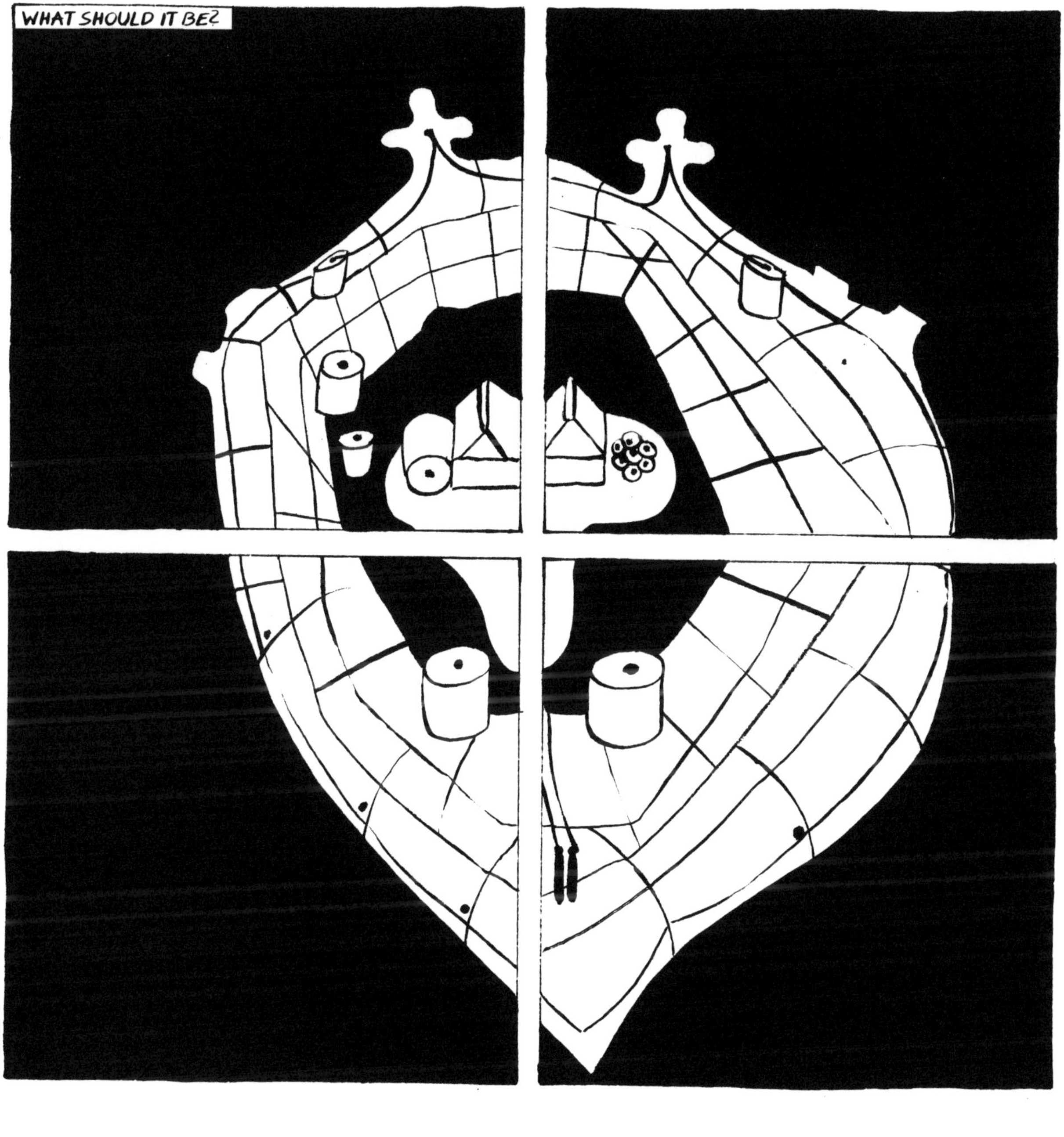
WHAT SHOULD IT BE?

* Quotes on pages 55, 90, 104, 114, 116, and 117 are from the play *Schlachten!* by Tom Lanoye and Luk Perceval based on the Wars of the Roses plays by William Shakespeare, in translation. Program book for the Salzburg Festival and the Deutsches Schauspielhaus Hamburg, 1999.

The translation of this work was supported by a grant from the Goethe-Institut in the framework of the Books First program.

Library of Congress Cataloging-in-Publication Data

Names: Hofer, Regina, 1976– author, artist.
Title: Fat / Regina Hofer.
Other titles: Blad. English
Description: University Park, PA : The Pennsylvania State University Press/Graphic Mundi, [2020] | Translated from German.
Summary: "A narrative, in graphic novel form, of a young woman coming of age while struggling with an eating disorder and family dysfunction. Documents the author's battle with body dysmorphic disorder, anorexia nervosa, and bulimia, which plagued her from her childhood through to adulthood"— Provided by publisher.
Identifiers: LCCN 2020027353 | ISBN 9780271088075 (paperback ; alk. paper)
Subjects: MESH: Anorexia Nervosa | Bulimia Nervosa | Body Dysmorphic Disorders | Personal Narrative | Graphic Novel
Classification: LCC RC552.A5 | NLM WI 17 | DDC 616.85/262—dc23
LC record available at https://lccn.loc.gov/2020027353

graphic mundi
drawing our worlds together

Graphic Mundi is an imprint of The Pennsylvania State University Press.

Fat Copyright © 2021 The Pennsylvania State University
All rights reserved
Printed in China
Published by The Pennsylvania State University Press, University Park, PA 16802-1003

Translated by Natascha Hoffmeyer

Title of the original edition: *Blad*

Text and illustrations © 2018 Regina Hofer
© 2018 Luftschacht Verlag, Wien

English-language edition arranged through mundt agency, Düsseldorf

The Pennsylvania State University Press is a member of the Association of University Presses.

It is the policy of The Pennsylvania State University Press to use acid-free paper. Publications on uncoated stock satisfy the minimum requirements of American National Standard for Information Sciences—Permanence of Paper for Printed Library Material, ANSI Z39.48–1992.